THE HUMOR OF
JAMES BOSS

A COLLECTION OF 400 JOKES

JAMES BOSS

The James Boss collection of humor books is an
excellent source for anyone needing entertainment
material. There are more than 30 books of humor in
the series so far. This book is a collection of
interactive jokes from several books already
published in New Zealand and online in shorter
forms.

INTRODUCTION

As Christmas entertainment, humor is the best. When you invite family, friends and colleagues to dinner this Christmas, make sure you have some surprises for your entertainment.

The interactive jokes in the James Boss books is designed to entertain, educate and provoke thinking about issues that are important to us all. Politics, education, social problems, smoking, alcoholism and so on are just some of the few addressed by the James Boss collection of jokes so far.

In this book, a collection of 300 is presented for your entertainment and those closest to you.

Simply read out each joke and invite everyone, in turn, to make a funny comment about it. This interaction brings out the groups wit and serious discussion of important issues in the jokes.

Enjoy

JOKE 1.

Australians have been calling Kiwis, the 'dole bludgers' for years. Recently, a prominent Australian TV commentator referred to the New Zealand Black Caps as the 'Bludging Army' before the final of the 2015 Cricket World Cup. It caused a huge scrap between the media of the 2 countries. One Kiwi retorted....'and the Aussies are bludging off God's sunshine, rain and natural resources....that's why they have too much money!'.

COMMENTS.

Dole bludgers refer, in New Zealand and Australia, to people who are on a welfare benefit....especially the unemployed. Complainants think they should look for a job. There are 500,000 Kiwis in Australia, according to media reports. Australians claim most of them are on the benefit.

JOKE 2.

A man who's name was stolen by a woman, decided to raid her bank account to draw attention to her trickery. Unfortunately for him, he got arrested by the Police for using her name!

COMMENTS:

The humor is in the arrest.   Obviously, she was using a man's name.

A satirical comment on the 'intelligence' of the Police.

JOKE 3.

A woman who was using a man's name came through the airport. The Customs Officer said, 'Madam, are you male or female?'. She said. 'I am a female, can't you see my female bits?'. 'Well, it is a man's name...you just have male boobs!....next".

COMMENTS:

Another satirical comment, poking fun at women who use male names.

JOKE 4.

A Police investigation was cancelled by the Minister after the suspect turned out to be Noah. 'Noah who?', enquired another Minister during their Cabinet Meeting....'Er well, you know...the one and only Noah!.... and the Ark?'.

COMMENT:

Another funny comment about the 'sometimes mistaken identities' that lead the Police to arrest the wrong people. Many New Zealanders have been granted 'millions of dollars' in compensation due to Police 'mistaken identities...or just mistakes'.

JOKE 5.

A speeding motorist was stopped by Police. The Officer suspected drugs. 'What kind of drug are you on, Sir?'....he asked the driver.

'Panadol Officer', came the reply.

COMMENT:

Another 'mistaken episode'...drugs suspected by the Police usually refer to hard drugs like marijuana, cocaine, heroine and so on. Not the drugs from the Doctors.

JOKE 6.

The Kingdom of Tonga has the most innovative export scheme in the Pacific. The country plan to export all its 100,000 citizens overseas.

COMMENT:

Tonga has 100,000 citizens in Tonga and about 200,000 Tongans living overseas. The country makes about $300-$500 million every year from remittances from overseas Tongans and only $60 million in exports. Therefore, 'one local concluded'.... it makes more sense to export the population!

JOKE 7.

A Kiwi was rushed to the Auckland Hospital after the Black Caps lost to the Aussies in the final of the 2015 Cricket World Cup. 'What seems to be the problem?', asked the Doctor. His Kiwi mate said...'drinking too much piss bro....he passed out'. The Doctor....who just emigrated to New Zealand wrote on his pad...."Seen patient...passed out from accidentally drinking too much urine".

COMMENT:

A humorous reference to the sometimes mistaken meaning of the 'slang' word for beer used by some kids. Piss is known only to a lot of people as urine, but to some local Kiwi kids...piss is beer!

JOKE 8.

A man tried to act out a Superman scene from his movie. He put on a Superman costume and jumped off the house roof. He landed on the driveway and passed out. When the neighbours asked....his 5 year old son said....'Daddy is dreaming of being superman!'.

COMMENT:

The humour is in the 'dreaming of being superman' comment. The kid obviously don't realise his Daddy has passed out!.

JOKE 9.

Rumor on Facebook suggest that Samoa owes more than $1 billion in debts. A creative local suggest they cede the country to China as a solution.

Another local said, 'Look mate....we don't want to give away the country...let's just ask Baycorp if we can pay it off....you know....weekly'.

COMMENT:

Baycorp is a debt collecting company in New Zealand well known to Pacific Islanders. The humor is the 'weekly repayment' of the billion dollars....some people sometimes don't realise it is a very big amount!

JOKE 10.

'America is at war with terror'....announced a radio news programme in New Zealand. A local quipped....'that's why Fonterra cannot export to America'.

COMMENT:

Most people in New Zealand have heard of the 'war on terror'. They have also heard of the 'difficulty' New Zealand face in exports to the United States since New Zealand's 'nuclear free' stance in 1984. Fonterra is the biggest exporter of dairy products from New Zealand. It is a satirical remark due to the 'similarity' of the sounds in 'terror' and 'Fonterra'.

JOKE 11.

Psychologists say, "Insane people think they have something to teach the world". A student questioned it during the lecture. "What about the lecturers?. Are they crazy?. They seem to think they have something to teach the world".

COMMENT: Often contradiction is the source of the humor. In this case an imaginary scene, but based on real events. The question posed by the student is the focus of the satirical point.

The humor is the apparent "ridiculousness" of the claim as many people would like to teach the world what they know. Or tell the world their story. People like Buddha, Confucious and Gandhi are examples.

JOKE 12.

A Mail Order company was asked if they have any adult literature. "Yes", the receptionist answered. "We sell all adult toys as well". "Can you sent me an adult female doll?. And send the bill to me?", the customer said. "Yes, Sir", it will be in the mail tomorrow". Next day the customer got a package with the bill. It has one item, "Dummy" with $100 cost and postage.

COMMENT: There are many companies that market their products or services based on the assumption that all their customers are dummies. I always watch some of the outrageous things they do to their customers in a New Zealand TV programme called "Fair Go". Recently, there was a complaint about a company charging their customers 4 times the price for their electricity or similar service. It is all a bit of fun in their eyes.

JOKE 13.

A wife and husband were in counselling for constant arguments at home. "He is stupid, he should get a job", she says. "What about you?", said the counsellor to the wife. "I have a job. I am an escort", says the wife.

COMMENT: Pacific women are well known for being very vocal to the point of being arrogant. In some cases the wife beats up the husband verbally everyday, on small things like vacuuming the house or washing the dishes. The humor here is the obvious outrageous arrangement they have.

JOKE 14.

A man ordered a cake from a cake shop. He went to pick it up in the afternoon. "How much is it?", he asked. "The ingredients are $50, the decoration $50, the base $10, the aroma $100, the aesthetic features $150, the mental picture $1,000 and the unforgettable occasion $1 million", the baker said. And how much is the recipe?", the man enquired. "That will be $1 billion, Sir", the baker said. "In that case, I will just have the ingredients", the man laughed.

COMMENT: A typical island joke.

JOKE 15.

A first time property investor asked the vendor if he can have the house and pay him with a "rent-to-own" arrangement. "Yeah, that's great", said the vendor. "On one condition. Have you got a $500,000 deposit?".

COMMENT: The vendor or owner of the house is just pulling the buyer's leg. The average house price in Auckland   is $500,000!.

JOKE 16.

A comedian was doing his stand up comedy routine. He was booed by the audience. "Why are you booing me?. I am the funniest Kiwi comedian around here", he asked. "We only like Kiwi comedians who make fun of Australians", a guy in the audience shouted.

COMMENT: There is an ongoing rivalry between New Zealanders and Australians. It started between the sports teams like rugby, league and cricket and seems to include jokes as well. There are many New Zealand jokes aimed at Australians.

JOKE 17.

"I am going to London for a holiday", said the wife. "What about me?", said the husband. "Just wait til I get to London and I will send you my address. You can come when you get organised", she said. Two weeks later, the husband got the address. It was "Tree No.19, Sherwood Forest, England".

COMMENT: A typical island joke.

This is a satirical joke about Europeans whom Pacific Islanders thought were all millionaires when they first came to the islands. It was only later that they discovered that some Europeans do live on the street.

JOKE 18.

New Zealand used to have an Alien Policy called the Alien Act 1948. Whenever Aliens land from Outer Space, they have to report to the local Police Station.

COMMENT: I first heard of this New Zealand Government Policy on TV and could not believe it. I think it has more to do with foreigners during World War II rather than Aliens from space.

JOKE 19.

A man was looking for a job. Finally he got an interview and was told to start the following week. Two days after, they rang again. "Is that Noah?. You were supposed to work for us next week?", the caller asked. "Yes", Noah answered. "We'll, we got your Conviction Record from the Ministry of Justice. You have 140 convictions for abusing animals on the ark. So I am very sorry but you cannot work for us".

COMMENT: This is another satirical joke

about the problem of convictions in New Zealand. Once you have a conviction or criminal record however minor, it is very difficult to find any company that will employ you. The cost of housing and feeding unemployed people in New Zealand cost billions of dollars each year, and this is one reason why some people are not employed.

JOKE 20.

A fake Policeman was working 11pm-7am as a Security Guard in a bank. The bank was robbed of $12,000 during the night. "What were you doing?", asked the Bank Manager. "We got robbed and you don't know anything".
"Sir, I did see the robbery. But I was outside and I cannot do anything. The robbers were in the bank and they were wearing Angel uniforms, so I started praying and God recalled them".

COMMENT: The Pacific is full of jokes about stupidity and this is one of them.

JOKE 21.

A man got a call from Baycorp. "Can you please confirm your birthday?", said the debt collecting agent. "No, I don't like giving personal details to strangers on the phone", the man said. "Can you confirm your birthday please?", the debt collector insisted. "Alright, it's the 99th of December 1884", the man answered.

COMMENT: Another satirical joke about stupidity. It also points out the problem of giving personal information to strangers on the phone. Many legitimate companies, in New Zealand, use the phone like Baycorp which is a debt collecting company, but it is time they come up with a better way of collecting their customers bad debts.

JOKE 22.

Definition of capital punishment according to Pinky of Otara. Capital punishment is when the Government gives you capital to start a business and then ensures it fails.

COMMENT: 95% of new businesses in New Zealand fail within 2 years. Many of them borrow some of the money to operate the business. This is a satirical comment about the stupidity of it all. Many of the companies which failed were due to bad debts, but you cannot force anyone in New Zealand to pay you without huge legal expenses. Even the products supplied by those failed companies are now supplied by foreign competitors.

JOKE 23.

Advise to Investors in New Zealand after 33 Finance Companies failed within 2 years of each other. "If you are making a lot of money, do not give it to the thieves to look after".

COMMENT: The Global Financial crisis was blamed for the failure of these 33 Finance companies losing $NZ5,000,000,000 of customers fund's. It is interesting that such huge amounts of money can just disappear into thin air. The joke is about the ridiculousness of the whole situation. There must be a thief somewhere.

JOKE 24.

Modern business is when you pay the top guy $20,000 a day and negotiate with the bottom guy to lower his fee from $100 to $50 a day.

COMMENT: It is unbelievable how some Chief Executive Officers can be paid $20,000 a day plus bonuses while some companies try to reduce the laborers wages to below the poverty line.

JOKE 25.

Notice at a Self-Employment Conference. "A man who works for himself is worth 1,000 in the workforce".

COMMENT: When there are no jobs around, the man with ideas and enthusiasm will always start his own business. Those with no skills and confidence end up in the welfare queues.

It is also true that the man who works for himself is the same one employing everyone else.

JOKE 26.

Notice at a Self-Improvement Conference. "Poor people are often snookered by their own negative attitudes".

COMMENT: This is very true. If you have worked with people who do not have any skills or enthusiasm and complain all the time....you will quickly see why they are in that situation. Many poor people in the world are prevented from getting ahead in life by their own negative attitudes.

The humor is in the ridiculousness   of it all. First World countries often spent billions in the Third World and getting no where because the locals don't know what they want to do!

JOKE 27.

Notice at a "Black Only" Conference. "A racist is a white person who is black inside".

COMMENT: This is a funny comment about racism. Satirical if you like. Discrimination is a worldwide problem. It is not bad as some people think but it requires education.

If people come from other countries with bad habits that you don't like....you will discriminate against them. You won't want to employ them, live near them, socialize with them or have anything to do with them. It is only when you get to know them or learn about their cultures and backgrounds that barriers can be broken down, then suddenly you find they are not so bad after all.

JOKE 28.

Notice at a Mechanics Conference. "Dirty hands are better than dirty minds".

COMMENTS: I love to fix cars and machines but I hate the black oil and grease on my hands that are hard to wash off. It put me off becoming a mechanic or an engineer. I used to watch my aunt's husband fix cars and vehicles since I was a child and really enjoy seeing him fix them.

The humor is in the "dirty mind" which is a humorous expression about people who are constantly thinking about naked women or sex all the time.

JOKE 29.

Notice at a Parents Convention. "Never scold your children for their faults. They got them from you".

COMMENT: I like a comment by Muhammad Ali. He said, "A country is judged by the way it treats its children"...or something similar. It is true kids learn a lot of bad habits from their parents.

The humor is in posting the statement at the the Parent's Convention. Its almost like a kid posted it there for parents to see.

JOKE 30.

Notice at a Sharemarket Meeting, "An Insider Trader is someone who knows what he is doing NOT the legality of his actions".

COMMENT: I saw a legal action being filed against a US Sharetrader on the TV news.

I thought about this humorous comment, the defence should claim that it was an "honest" mistake.

JOKE 31.

Notice at a Pastor's Meeting. "People who tell lies have nothing else in their heads".

COMMENT: There are some people who are compulsive liars. You always find it hard to believe anything they say.

The humor is in referring to liars as "empty heads". There is nothing else in their heads but lies.

JOKE 32.

A man was fishing in the South Island. The God Maui appeared to him. "Have you got anything yet?". "No", the man answered. "Just move the waka a bit closer to Australia and hook the Great Barrier reef", Maui said. "Don't you think it's a bit too big?", the man said. "Our waka might sink".

COMMENT: A typical Pacific joke. Maui is one of the Polynesian Gods. He is credited with fishing most of the Pacific Islands, including the South and North Islands of New Zealand, out of the sea. In New Zealand, the North Island is called "Te Ika a Maui" or Maui's fish and the South Island "Te Waka a Maui" or Maui's boat.

JOKE 33.

A cow ran away from a farm in the Waikato. She met up with a bull in Hastings. After a few drinks, the bull said. "My dear, shall we go to your farm or mine?".

COMMENT: A different version of an old joke. The joke is about a boy taking out a girl and asking her "Your place or mine" after.

Another version is a reference to a Prince and Princess. "Your Palace or mine?".

The humor is that this time its a bull and cow doing it.

JOKE 34.

An insurance man was cold calling in Auckland. He was advertising funeral insurance. The first customer asked a question. "So you propose to give me the best burial in the whole town?". "Yes, Madam", he said. "Why don't you give me the money so I can enjoy it while I am still alive?", she says.

COMMENT: An insurance broker once rang me and offered me the best funeral in town. I thought it was a joke, but it was not. There are also a lot of insurance companies offering the same service on New Zealand Television. It appears that funerals are big business.

The joke is poking ridicule at the business of paying for a great funeral while you   still have time on earth. Some people think it's a great idea.

JOKE 35.

Three kids were playing in a backyard. "My dad can beat your Dads. He is a boxer", said the first kid. "No, my Dad is stronger. He is a weight lifter", said the 2nd kid. "No, my Dad is stronger. He can cheat your Dads anytime. He is a Lawyer", said the 3rd kid.

COMMENT: Obvious just a satirical joke about lawyers. I have not come across any bad lawyers, but I could not resist this one. I thought it is funny. "Brains vs Brawns".

JOKE 36.

A family went for a holiday in Wellington. They finally arrived at the Beehive in the afternoon. Miss Five asked. "Wow, what a large beehive. Are there any bees inside Mum?". "Yes honey. They are called Politicians", Mum laughed.

COMMENT: Kids say the darnest things sometimes. The Parliament building of New Zealand is called the Beehive because it looks like a giant beehive.

The humor is obviously the question of whether there are any "bees" inside the Beehive.

JOKE 37.

A Kiwi praises the good points of migrating to New Zealand to some Islanders. "You know in New Zealand, even if you are a criminal you can still be an Honourable Member of Parliament".

COMMENT: There was some furore in New Zealand about a certain Member of Parliament who had a drink driving conviction. The joke is ridiculing the system where people who cannot get jobs because they have a criminal conviction can still be a Member of Parliament.

JOKE 38.

Two businessmen were talking in an Auckland bar. "You know 95% of all business startups fail in the first 2 years", said the first businessman. "Yeah, I was wondering why we have a $700 million trade deficit in the last quarter", said the second businessman.

COMMENT: A satirical joke ridiculing the inability of the system to correct this very obvious economic problem in New Zealand.

JOKE 39.

Pinky of Otara has suggested that the Police reopen the case of Cain murdering Abel for further investigation.

COMMENT: Just poking ridicule at recent Police investigation mistakes that resulted in many innocent people ending in jail for up to 13 years!

JOKE 40.

Doctors have reported 2 new diseases in New Zealand. The first one is, "back to work syndrome" which attack Kiwis on Mondays. The second one is, "budget syndromes" which attack Kiwis on Saturdays.

COMMENTS: A funny joke about an age old Kiwi complaint that it is really hard to go back to work after such a nice week end.

A Kiwi is an endangered native bird of New Zealand....and New Zealanders are usually referred to as Kiwis.

JOKE 41.

A business owner complained to his wife that somebody is robbing him at work. "Who do you work with?", the wife asked. "We'll, there is Mrs Robinson, and Robyn Honey", he said. "Have you got anyone called Robbing Boss at work?", the wife asked.

COMMENT: Just a humorous comment about English names.

JOKE 42.

A University student was doing a project on the origin of names, including names of days and months. He claims that Friday was named after Friday Crusoe, son of Robinson Crusoe.

COMMENT: A humorous joke about the character "Friday" in the famous novel "Robinson Crusoe".

JOKE 43.

A man was wrongly convicted and put in the crazy house. He found it very boring so he decided to do some courses by correspondence. He did a Bachelor of Arts, then a Master of Arts, then a PhD. The Doctor concluded he is not crazy and released him. He also asked the Government for $1 million compensation and got it.   When he got home his Mum asked. "Where have you been in the last 8 years?. He told his Mum what happened. "Oh my God", she says. "We should send everyone to the crazy house!".

COMMENT: A humorous joke about the mistake of sending some "bright" people to the crazy house.

JOKE 44

Doctors have a drinking problem. They don't drink at all.

JOKE 45

A psychologist reported to his Board that his

patients have no drinking problem at all. They are drinking heaps of beer.

JOKE 46

Protesters campaigning against a proposed local liquor shop. "Drink   Coke   not Piss".

JOKE 47

A job interviewer asked a job applicant. "Do you drink at all?".
"Yes", he says.
"What do you drink?", she asked.
"Water", was the answer.

JOKE 48

An alcoholic ran off with a carton of beer from a liquor shop. The Police gave chase but he drank all the beer while running. It was all finished when he was caught. The Police took samples to prove he drank the beer and he was taken to court. The judge let him off saying, "the sample does not smell or taste like beer".

JOKE 49

Alcoholic Anonymous advertised for a new Manager. The only condition was he should able "to drink everyone under the table".

JOKE 50

Pretty girls like wise men who take them to dinner and buy them a glass of wine. After a few bottles they can ride off into the sunset.

JOKE 51

Health Professionals swear by the health benefits of red wine. Drinking red wine in moderation lowers your cholesterol, improves your attitude, increase your life expectancy and will make you as randy as a goat.

JOKE 52

Job Advert outside a pub. "Drinkers required. Must be able to drink one carton at one sitting".

JOKE 53

Germans are reputed to drink more beer than any other nation. They average 2 liters each per week. Some Kiwis protested, they drink 10 liters of   beer each,   in New Zealand. They said.

JOKE 54

In a recent survey of beer drinkers across Europe. Traditional drinkers who have a "beer gut" say they are not obese just "stout".

JOKE   55

Samoans are world famous alcoholics. They drink "a   beer"   everyday.

JOKE 56

Queen Victoria   of the United Kingdom and Empress of India   was reported to have a "pint" with her breakfast every morning.   It was not a drinking problem.

JOKE 57

Olympic fans say that watching the Olympiads at the London Olympics put them in the mood. They are faster, stronger, prettier, sexier and makes them drink more.

JOKE 58

New Police advise to drink drivers. "Crash in bed instead of the road".

JOKE 59

Japanese farmers feed beer to their cattle to "generate fat infusion" in the steak and make it taste better. It is also reported that it puts the ladies in the mood after a premium steak dinner and wine.

JOKE   60

During one of the pub crawls in their school days, two mates were talking in the pub. I don't like people "bullshitting me", the first one said. "Yeah right, I prefer people pissing me", the other mate replied and he took off to the toilet.

JOKE 61

Bits of Wisdom in the local newspaper. "If you want the special lady in your life to say yes all the time, give her 3 glasses of wine before dinner".

JOKE 62

It is common wisdom that women look more beautiful after a few drinks. "That is why some married   men drink a lot", says the AA advisor.

JOKE 63

Women are like fine wines. They get better with age, says one friend. The other disagreed, "mate my wife's punches are harder as she gets older. She knocked me out cold last Friday when I returned home at 3am".

JOKE 64

Researchers have found that alcohol is

actually good for you. Drinking beer improves digestion and general health. It is high in flavonoids which are natural anti-oxidants. It also helps the drinkers "get it up" all the time.

JOKE 65

Wedding parties in the outback in Australia were famous years ago. After each party the Groom usually goes around in the morning and film everyone sleeping, under trees, in the garage, on the ute and even in the swimming pool!, basically dropping where they stood.

JOKE 66

Alcohol is more commonly known as Ethanol to chemists. Some people in the South Pacific used to make homebrew from yeast, sugar and water. Sometimes they feel sick the next day, after drinking it. Local Chemists say they must be producing more "methanol" than ethanol in their brew.

JOKE 67

During the "prohibition" in the United States, alcohol was distilled and brewed in secret. It was then sold by the "bootleggers" in the black market. It was the cocaine of those years. Futurologists say that in as little as 50 years, they will be selling cocaine, heroine and marijuana in the supermarkets.

JOKE 68

After a rugby tour for a pre-season game in Hamilton, the Auckland players drove back in their bus and stopped at every pub on the way. They have a beer jug skulling competition, then a vomiting competition in the back of the bus. Then sang "we wanna wiwi" now the rest of the way.

JOKE 69

The Coach of the Auckland team says later "its all part of fun for the boys. I told them it's alright but no pissing on the seats".

JOKE 70

Alcohol is only a problem when you crave for it all the time, and you are drunk all the time. That causes problems like conflict with others, says the AA consultant. "Yeah, but I only drink like 2 boxes of beer a week", says the client.

JOKE 71

The New Zealand Parliament recently voted to leave the drinking age at 18. Raising it to 20 will not change anything. Critics say "it's a bit unusual that you can drive a car at 16 but cannot consume alcohol until 18".

JOKE 72

A drunk driver was arrested for "zigzagging" on the road. His school mate, the judge led him off. "Apparently there is a loophole in the law. Zigzagging on the road is not an offence", he concluded.

JOKE 73

Two criminals were in the "holding room" in the court waiting to be tried. They were arrested for being "drunk and disorderly". The police officer came around with the menu for lunch. "What do you want?. We have pizza, pies and sandwiches". "Just leave the tray officer, we are bit hungry", they replied. "Choice bro! This is the best restaurant in town". One said to the other after the officer left.

JOKE 74

The Surgeon General has advised that smoking causes anxiety, depression, sterility, emphysema, bronchitis, rotten teeth, bad breath, many other diseases and stupidity.

JOKE 75

John Rambo, of the Rambo movie fame, says he is dumping his smoking girlfriend because "her farts smell of cigarettes".

JOKE 76

Ciggy Quinncalnut quit smoking because
Doctors did some tests of his blood and found
all 200 poisons in it.

JOKE 77

Kok One says his girlfriend gave up smoking
"because she cannot fit any more of my
cigarettes in it".

JOKE 78

Famous All Black Smokin Joe Stanley was
asked where he got the smokin from. He says
he got it from the "secondhand smoke in the
pub".

JOKE 79

According to Statistics, most boyfriends
dump their smoking girlfriends because "they
crave it more than me".

JOKE 80

Tobacco Companies say smoking is just another risk. Like a car crash, falling off a skyscraper, eaten by a shark or being shot in the lungs.

JOKE 81

One of the techniques for quitting smoking is to list your priorities. If smoking is not a priority, you have to give it up. However, most smokers list smoking as one of the most important items in the shopping list.

JOKE 82

Your brain is in control when you smoke. It puts value on the 'feel good factor'. Once the brain rejects cigarettes, you will find it offensive. Try this exercise. Always think your cigarette is a piece of crap and see what happens after a few weeks.

JOKE 83

U.S. Army advisors have advised the

Pentagon to give free marijuana to the terrorists "to drive them nuts". It's cheaper than shooting them.

JOKE 84

Susan of Otara says her neighbour was rushed to hospital for "smoking angel mushroom by mistake". He was out of cigarettes and had no money to buy any.

JOKE 85

Lee O Nut, famous British journalist, has quit smoking. He just discovered that newspaper ink is poisonous.

JOKE 86

The Red Indians used tobacco as a "peace pipe". It is now being used in the Third World to eradicate the poor.

JOKE 87

American smokers now prefer to smoke the deer they hunt instead of themselves.

JOKE 88

Kiwis are going to follow the American example by smoking Eels.

JOKE 89

Aussies will copy the Kiwis by smoking Matilda.

JOKE 90

The Otara Activists Group says the cigarette companies have deep pockets. If we sue them for cigarette damage to our people and the environment we will all be rich.

JOKE 91

New Zealand MP Tariana Turia says cigarettes kill 13 people every year, therefore it should be banned. Cigarette companies say if people want to kill themselves, it's a personal choice.

JOKE 92

Heller's sausages will introduce a "smoking sausage" for smokers. They say it will "fit perfectly in your mouth". Funny that.

JOKE 93

Protesters in the United States of America plan to contaminate tobacco plantations by "infecting the plants with dummy genes". They say it will turn smokers into dummies and serve as a deterrent.

JOKE 94

Smoking Protesters in New Zealand say "smoke seekiss" instead of "seegarats".

JOKE 95

"Buying cigarettes will cost you $1,500 a year if you smoke 2 packets a week", the Doctor said to the patient. "It's alright, I will just pinch them from the wife's packet. That will save me $1,500 a year", he says.

JOKE 96

The New Zealand Government report say that the Ministry of Health spend millions of dollars caring for people with smoking related illnesses. Smokers say it is a positive because it helps employ a lot of health workers.

JOKE 97

The best way to stop smoking is to find a better reason to quit. You don't need chewing gums, nicotine pads or hypnosis. My neighbour says she found a better reason. She will smoke marijuana instead of cigarettes.

JOKE 98

If you stop smoking your food will taste better, your bank account will be fatter, your breath will be fresh, your libido will be greater, says the brochure. "The only problem is, says the smoker, I have plenty of libido now but my wife has totally lost hers".

JOKE 99

Legend suggest that Columbus introduced cigarette smoking from the "new world" to the "old world". He liked the Red Indians "peace pipe" so much he smoked it every day.

JOKE 100

New Technologies are now available to people who cannot quit smoking. If all else fails, your Doctor can give you a "new brain from a non-smoker".

JOKE 101

Statistics suggest that low income earners are more likely to smoke than well to do people. Most of them started at school because it made them "look cool". But it not only empties their wallets it also stunted their brains.

JOKE 102

Fishermen in the city of New Plymouth will help the Ministry of Health with their new anti-smoking campaign. Their slogan is "Smoke fish not ciggies".

JOKE 103

Australia introduced "plain packaging" of cigarette packs to discourage new smokers. The next step would be to stop cigarette companies from putting any cigarettes inside the packs.

JOKE 104

An RIP Notice at Waikumete Cemetery in Auckland.

Here lies Gonago
Died from smoking Tobacco
Hailed from Tobago
Wife from Monaco

Started smoking at school
Brain stunted like a fool
Disobeyed the rules
'Cos he thought it was cool

He was only 46 years old

Lost his warmth in the cold
Which made him smoke more
And got sicker than before

Now he is in heaven
Like Noah's raven
He flew into a smoking port
And never left, now he is with God.

JOKE 105

A writer wrote 120 books but his boss keeps stealing them. Finally, out of frustration, he says 'Boss stop stealing my books!'...the Boss thought for a moment and he said...'Ok, don't worry I will pay you back'...the writer retorted....'But that's what you said about my wages, 20 years ago...and you haven't paid yet!'.

JOKE 106

During rugby practise one day a first fifteen team was going through its moves. The first five was a new guy. The Coach instructed him to kick the ball to the box when he gets it from the half-back. "Where's the box Coach?

I don't see any", he says.

JOKE 107

A school which entered the inter-school competition for the first time was learning some new moves. The winger would come in and take the ball off the first five and pass it to the full back who will follow him. On game day the full back was injured and had to stand on the sideline with the reserves. The winger was not aware of it. When the move was called he came in took the ball off the first five, ran across to the sideline and pass it to the injured full back.

JOKE 108

Andy Haden was well known for winning a certain game for Auckland against Wellington. What was his favourite jump called?
ANS: A sidestep.

JOKE 109

"Inga the   winger" is well known as a hard and fast runner of the ball. What is he most

famous for?"
ANS: Burying the opposition.

JOKE 110

Jonah Lomu became a Rugby Superstar
during the 1995 Rugby World Cup in South
Africa.
What do you call the opposition tackling
Jonah Lomu?
ANS: A hospital pass.

JOKE 111

Wayne Shelford was famous as the only All
Black captain who did not lose a game. He is
also famous for another reason in a game
against France. What was it?
ANS: He played the full game with a cracked
ball.

JOKE 112

Tonga is one of the developing teams in world
rugby. It is often referred to as one of the
minnows at world cup time. During the last
world cup they beat one of the finalists.

Which one was it?
ANS: The Cocks (more commonly known as the Roosters/France).

JOKE 113

The Manu Samoa played the All Blacks in 1992, at Mt Smart Stadium, for the first time. They were beaten by which pass?
ANS: The "some more" pass.

JOKE 114

The All Blacks played the Polynesian 15 for the first time in 1999. What were they called?
ANS: The All Browns

JOKE 115

During the Springbok Tour in 1981. New Zealand was divided over the apartheid policy of the South African Government. Thousands of Protestors clashed with Police outside each venue. On the last game day at Eden Park thousands of protesters clashed with Police outside. Many were inside throwing smoke bombs into the field which was surrounded with razor wire. During the game a small plane was dropping nails on the field. The game was halted while they pick up the nails. The plane came back, chased by a Police helicopter, and dropped what on to the field? It was called a Knight raid.

ANS: It dropped flour bombs on to the field. One hit Gary Knight (All Black prop) on the head and had to be carried out of the field.

JOKE 116

Rugby games are sometimes won in the last minute with a penalty kick or drop goal. What girl drives the rugby players crazy in the last minute?
ANS: The curl of the banana kick.

JOKE 117

The All Blacks are also well known for their fearsome haka. What do you call a shaking boot?
ANS: The opposition during the haka.

JOKE 118

Jonah Lomu became famous instantly in the 1995 World Cup for his first try. Why did Jonah Lomu ran over the cat?
ANS: Because he lost his nine lives.

JOKE 119

Which All Black is well known for smoking the opposition?
ANS: Smokin   Joe Stanley

JOKE 120

What is Rugby's   most famous restaurant in Auckland?
ANS: Eat   n   Park

JOKE 121

What do you call a whitewash?
ANS: The All Blacks beating England.

JOKE 122

What do you call an All Black   snack?

ANS: A Wallaby

JOKE 123

What do you call an All Black maul?
ANS: A Carter Pillar

JOKE 124

Which All Black is most famous for foxing
the opposition?
ANS: Grant Fox

JOKE 125

What do you call an All Black   Tua?
ANS: A left hook

JOKE 126

Which All Black is most famous for keeping
the opposition depressed?
ANS: JK

JOKE 127

What do you call the All Blacks passing the

ball around?
ANS: A donate O

JOKE 128

Rugby players are also famous for romance.
What is a rugby player's favourite line?
ANS: The tryline

JOKE 129

What do you call an All Black attack?
ANS: A hurry can

JOKE 130

What do you call a blackout?
ANS: The All Blacks keeping Australia at 0.

JOKE 131

What did the buck say to the marmite?
ANS: My mites are bigger than yours.

JOKE 132

Which pole is rugby player's most famous for

expeditions to?
ANS: The pole on the opposition tryline

JOKE   133

What is a BBcue?
ANS: Bring Back Buck

JOKE 134

What is a rugby player's goal in life?
ANS: Scoring goals

JOKE   135

What is the most used phrase during rugby
meals?
ANS: Pass the bowl

JOKE 136

What follows a jug skulling competition
during an aftermatch?
ANS: The song "We wanna wiwi now".

JOKE 137

Coach: "Ok, boys let's start with a run around the paddock to warm up before training".

Hooker: "I'm already warm coach, I have 2 jumpers on".

JOKE 138

Club Manager: "We are investing some of our funds for future security of the club".

Half-Back: "Can you tell us how much is a 50% investment, Sir".

JOKE 139

Coach: "Listen up boys, here's the game plan. As soon as the opposition gets the ball you put pressure on the first five".

New Supporter: "How about they put pressure on more players Coach, who's going to pressure the other 10?'.

JOKE 140

Club Captain: "Thank you everyone for your support during our fundraiser last week. Somebody say grace before we eat please".

Senior Team Winger: "Amazing grace how sweet the sound, That saved a wing like me..."

JOKE 141

Club Fundraiser: "During the prize giving we will need a clown to wear a suit and entertain the kids. I need a volunteer"

Senior Team Captain: "How about the fullback, Sir?"

JOKE 142

Coach: "I want the tight-five to make sure our scrum does not collapse"

Locks: "Don't worry Coach we have Armstrong boots on".

JOKE 143

First-five: "12-19-22"

Second-five: "What move is that?"

JOKE 144

Hooker: "12-19-22"

Opposition First five to Second five: "Watch it he is throwing the ball to the backs!"

JOKE 145

Coach: "In this move, the tight five pushes their forwards back as the ball carrier breakaway and fall on the line".

Flanker: "Is that going to be me Sir?".

JOKE 146

Rugby Supporter: "Our team is playing Georgia in the Rugby World Cup next week"

Tennis Player: "I am playing Georgina next

week, as well".

JOKE 147

All Black Supporter: "Our team won 42 of its last 47 games"

Wallaby Supporter: "Our team won its last game in Sydney against the All Blacks".

JOKE 148

All Black Supporter: "The All Blacks   has won more games against Australia".

Wallaby Supporter: "The Kangaroos has won more games against the Kiwis"

JOKE 149

All Black Supporter: "We are going to win this world cup".

Wallaby Supporter: "We are winning the next world cup".

JOKE 150

Rugby Tourist to England: "Excuse me, can you show us the road to the town of Football?".

Tourist Guide: "Sorry, the name of the town is Rugby, not Football".

JOKE 151

Jihadi John and the terror assassins shown on TV are always dressed in black and the victims are always in orange. Anyone has any ideas? Jihadi John used to live in London. His family still flats over there!

JOKE 152

The $US 25 million price of Salman Rusdie's head is the biggest ever offered for the assassination of a human being. And what did he do? He wrote a book that was critical of Islam! He is said to be a Moslem! Whos fighting who?

JOKE 153

There are 80 million Iranians shouting 'death to America and Israel' on the streets and there is just one response from the Allies. Ban Iran from making any nuclear bombs, but they can buy it from anyone offering.

JOKE 154

Since the Allied sanctions against Iran were put in place, independent protesters claim that Iran now has more war planes and bombs than before! They bought them from the Russians!

JOKE 155

Europe's open door policy to war refugees from the Middle East has been blamed for the recent bombings in Paris. Now they are shutting the door on refugees, the bombers are moving to Washington.

JOKE 156

A terrible picture of a hand and fingers that

was mutilated with perhaps more than 100 hundred cuts appeared on Facebook. The claim was it belonged to a Moslem person who read the bible and was punished for it. It is interesting that Islam accept Moses, the prophets and Jesus Christ as part of their religion but Moslems cannot read the bible without a 'near death' punishment!.

JOKE 157

The list of co-lateral damage in the war increase every year. More arms for Iran from Russia, more money for Boko Haram for supporters, more innocent homeless people in the war in Syria, ISIS gets more money and volunteers, more commercial jet planes being shot down and so on.

JOKE 158

There are 30 million Moslems in China and about half that number in the United States according to many reports. That is already 45 million in just 2 countries! We don't hear anything about them at all. Have they heard of the war?

JOKE 159

The list of beneficiaries in the Middle East conflict is a long one. Secure oil supplies, arms sales increase, better funding for the armies, increased news revenue, more donations for charity, kudos for the Allies, more funding for Israel, improved technology in the West and so on.

JOKE 160

New Rugby Supporter to friend: "My son is the third-five in their team"

Friend: "My sons are first-five and second-five in their team"

JOKE 161

The Allies strategy for the war. 1. Isolate Iran and the terrorist and destroy them. 2. Make the oil supplies for the world secure 3. Sell more arms to the terrorists. 4. Make friendly gestures towards non-participating Moslem countries in trade and international co-operation.

JOKE 162

The terrorist strategy for this war. 1. Increase their share of the land in Syria and Iraq. They currently hold a piece the size of Uganda with 20 million residents. 2. Get a British passport and accent 3. Sell more oil to the Allies 4. Ban Iran from joining the conflict

JOKE 163

Russia's plan for this conflict. 1. Sell more weapons, guns, bullets, planes to Iran. 2. Veto any interference from the Allies in the UN Security Council 3. Bomb American interference in the Middle East 4. Keep poor refugees out of Russia

JOKE 164

Europe's plan for this conflict. 1. Invite all poor Moslems and refugees to come to Europe and convert to Christianity 2. Employ all the newly invited citizens in European Industries and sell the products to USA, China and the Middle East including guns, bullets, planes, tanks, aircraft carriers, warships and so on.

JOKE 165

British plans for this conflict. 1. Ensure only the strongest refugees come to Britain to join the selection for the next rugby world cup team 2. Steal all good football players from broken villages and towns in the Middle East 3. Make the UK great again, in rugby and football 4. Try and deport Jihadi John

JOKE 166

The FIFA secret plans for this conflict. Arrange for all the sides to have a team in the next FIFA Soccer World Cup in Russia to decide who is the best team.

JOKE 167

The Kingdom of Tonga's plan for this conflict. 1. Soldiers to sing as many hymns as they can in the camps 2. Convert terrorists to Christianity through prayer 3. Invite the terrorists to come and buy a Tongan passport

JOKE 168

The Fijian plans for this conflict 1. Export as much yagona as possible to the Middle East 2. Ensure terrorists drink kava all night before any war engagements 3. Get the terrorists hooked on kava like the Australian aborigines 4. Get the Tongans to do the 'sipi tau' before the battle

JOKE 169

Samoa's plan for the war. 1. Still discussed in cabinet since 2001
2. Still praying on it since 2001
3. Still recruiting some soldiers since 2001

JOKE 170

All Black Fan: "I just bought the largest TV in the shops and setup a Sky account to watch the All Blacks win the Rugby World Cup".

Wallaby Fan: "I'll buy a bigger TV than yours to watch the Wallaby beat the All Blacks".

JOKE 171

England Fan: "This year England will win the Rugby World Cup for the third time".

All Black and Wallaby Fans: "Naah, second time!"

England Fan: "So you agree we have a better team?".

JOKE 172

Sign outside cafe in town of Rugby, England during Rugby World Cup:
"All Rugby Fans are Welcome".

JOKE 173

All Black Fan: "The All Blacks will surely beat all the other teams this year".

Wallaby Fan: "Nah, the Wallabies will beat all the other teams this year"

England Fan: "Nah, England will beat all the teams this year".

Tongan Fan: "I hope we can beat Georgia!".

JOKE 174

Sign outside Post Office in town of Rugby
during world cup:
"Put it between the posts, Johny".

JOKE 175

Sign outside a Theatre in England:
Try on our line. Shakespeare parts available.

JOKE 176

French Fan: "The French team is unbeatable
this year".

Welsh Fan: "Nah, Wales is unbeatable this
year".

Fijian Fan: "Fiji was unbeatable in the Pacific
Cup".

Manu Samoa Fan: "The Manu Samoa siva is
unbeatable this year".

JOKE 177

TV News Announcer: "The Rugby World Cup fever has hit London".

New fans watching TV: "What's the temperature?".

JOKE 178

Coach: "Alright boys, as soon as the ball comes out of the ruck pass it to the backs".

New Rugby Supporter: "It might be better to keep the ball at the front Coach. You are losing ground passing it to the back".

JOKE 179

Tongan Rugby Fan: "The 'Ikale Tahi is ready to do battle this year".

England Supporter: "What's that?".

Tongan Rugby Fan: "Sea Eagle".

England Supporter: "Would the Sea Eagle like

a Rose before dinner?"

JOKE 180

Sign outside rugby changing room:
"Keep this room clean or there will be some
hash climate changes in the rules!"

JOKE 181

All Black Fan: "Dan Carter is going to kick
the winning penalty in the world cup final".

England Fan: "Nah, its going to be Johny
Wikinson".

All Black Fan: "I thought he is retired".

England Fan: : "We'll recall him".

JOKE 182

Sign outside stadium during Rugby World
Cup:

Be quiet, penalty in progress.

JOKE 183

Referee: "Captain make sure your team behaves, no more spear tackles or you will get a red card".

Captain: "Hey Warriors, throw all your spears outside".

JOKE 184

All Black Fan: "We're singing Pokarekareana during the final".

Wallaby Fan: "We're singing Waltzing Matilda".

England Fan: "We're singing Swing Low".

Tongan Fan: "We hate singing or noisy fans during important games.

JOKE 185

According to common knowledge, cocaine is mostly supplied from South America. It has become the curse of many unemployed people in the United States. During one court case the prosecutor asked the defendant "You are listed as unemployed, yet you own several mansions, more than 10 flash cars and have many wives. Where did you get them from?.

"They are all provided by God Sir", replied the drug dealer.
COMMENT: The humour here is the obvious contradiction in the defendant's "unemployed status" and his wealth. It may have been an oversight on his part, but it suggests that his business is not registered and he does not pay any taxes.

The added comment by the defendant that they were provided by God is a funny but also a good discussion point.

JOKE 186

Al Capone was a notorious supplier of "bootleg" in the black market in Chicago. During an enforcement visit by 2 of his gangsters to a customer for non-payment, they entered the shop when the customer was preparing to cook a chicken. "Whatever you do to that chicken well do to you", they threatened. The customer picked up the chicken and kissed its backside.

COMMENT: We have all heard of the Al Capone story. The chicken part of the joke is something I read in a book a long time ago. The funny part is the "victim's" rebellion by kissing the chicken on the backside.

Those days are long gone and no one would suggest it is still going on in the United States, but I think it is a good discussion point…with some added humour.

JOKE 187

Yacht races in the Pacific are becoming more fashionable these days. Some yachts tend to "pickup cargo" on the way and still win the race. The first ones to arrive will circle around until the "winner" arrives.

COMMENT: I would not suggest there is a lot of cheating and drug dealing going on during yacht races, but it is one of those "imaginary jokes". The funny bit, of course, being the "cheating"…that the first to arrive would circle around until the "winner" crosses the finish line. People who watch a lot of the Captain Hook cartoons would understand this joke.

JOKE 188

The new world has many opportunities for many Island States. They can get a loan from the International Monetary fund, World Bank, Asian Development Bank, other countries and the Drug Cartels.

COMMENT: No one would suggest that Pacific Island countries are getting loans from Drug Cartels or that Drug Cartels do exist, but it is a bit like the previous joke. A Captain Hook situation if you like. It is also a kind of satire of the stupidity of such actions.

JOKE 189

Amphetamine Labs are springing up all over New Zealand according to the New Zealand Police. They cook the drugs and sell them for millions of dollars.

Users say the amphetamine gives you a high, makes you fat and mean then drops you like a stone.

COMMENT: The New Zealand TV news often shows the raids Police carry out on Amphetamine Labs. It is a very serious situation. The manufacturing process often leaves residues on the walls and other parts of the building that need to be cleaned. All personnel involved have to wear special clothing and wash up after. The residues must be very toxic…and are said to cause health problems to tenants after the drug dealers are gone.

COMMENT: The humour here is the "side effects" of the drugs on the users. They "become fat and drop like a stone". It is also very serious…users do lose their lives or become "a zombie" if they use the drug excessively.

JOKE 190

According to the New Zealand News, the entire Cabinet of the Tongan Government recently met a notorious drug dealer in his yacht , at Nuku'alofa wharf, to "arrange a loan".

COMMENT: I watched this news bulletin and thought it very odd for the Tongan Government to deal with drug dealers. I thought it must be a joke. However, it really shows the vulnerability of small nations who are sometimes tricked by drug dealers and other con men out of their hard earned cash and savings.

There is also a story about the Tongan Government "losing" $US27 million to an insurance conman in recent years. The conman was said to be the King's "joker" or entertainer!

JOKE 191

Drug money is faster than selling taro and coconuts observed a Tongan newspaper. "That's why we are breeding "marijuana cassava" to sell to the drug dealers around the world. No one will suspect a thing", says the informer.

COMMENT: Cassava leaves resemble marijuana leaves but are much larger. Cassava is a rootcrop and common staple food in the Pacific Islands and many other parts of the world. The joke is to breed cassava varieties with leaves that have the same "effect" as marijuana to "add value" to the local cassava varieties.

Sometime in the future this maybe acceptable with new technologies. When you can add value to a crop by breeding other "uses" into it.

JOKE 192

The United States and Japanese companies are making billions of dollars in China from the cheap labour available. This has left more than 20 million people unemployed and selling drugs in the United States, says the paper reports. The only "unemployed" people making money are the drug dealers.

COMMENT: The humour is the obvious contradiction between Americans making millions in China by employing cheap labour at the expense of Americans at home who cannot find jobs. This joke would probably pass as a Spike Milligan joke. He was a British entertainer.

This is a good discussion point because drug dealers tend to thrive in situations of high unemployment. They "pickup" a lot of   kids willing to sell drugs to make money.

JOKE 193

A labourer was asked for a sample by his boss, because they are now "drug testing" all their staff. The labourer put beer in the container and handed it back. Next day he was fired for being "drunk" during work time. There was a "lot of alcohol" in his urine.

COMMENT: Many employers resort to drug testing to stamp out drug use in their workplace. Obviously a drug user will try to avoid handing a sample in. The joke is the drug user handing in a "beer sample" and was fired because of its "high alcohol" content! He must have been stoned when he did it!

JOKE 194

Marijuana is being sold in Auckland for $20 a joint. Many labourers make $900 from selling marijuana and $163 from their jobs every 2 weeks.

COMMENT: This is just a joke aimed at the low wages labourers are being paid. They resort to selling drugs to supplement their income.

It is very real in some places. Some young men sell marijuana for $20 per joint…and make more money than their wages!

JOKE 195

In 50-100 years time supermarkets will be selling cocaine, heroine, marijuana and other drugs. It will probably in a different form from to-day, says the Otara Activist Group.

COMMENT: There is no such group called the Otara Activist group. It is a bit of humour about people in South Auckland being "egg-centric". But the point being made is a serious one. Like alcohol, one day hard drugs will also be available from the shops. New Zealand did allow the sale of synthetic drugs in the shops for a while but has decided to ban them again. Probably, from too many problems related to the use of these "recreational drugs".

JOKE 196

"If you sell drugs in the supermarkets that will kill our business", says a drug spokesperson. "We will march in protest". "I am sure the Police will welcome you marching on our main road", says his friend.

COMMENT: Can you imagine the drug dealers marching down your main road protesting against the destruction of their business? It might be a scene straight out of "The Simpsons".

JOKE 197

Police are fighting drug dealers in certain "slum areas" in South Auckland. They put cameras in their flats disguised as fire alarms.

The only problem is that, "after watching their women undress and make love hundreds of times, they have fallen in love with them", says a Police spokesperson.

COMMENT: It is possible for Police Officers who watch surveillance camera activity to be compromised in some way. But like Adam falling under the spell of Eve, it is only natural. Humans are made of flesh and blood and hormones that run out of control. Maybe the Police should design ways to avoid this from happening.

JOKE 198

In certain countries in Europe, you are allowed to keep a marijuana plant for your own consumption.
When the Police raided one flat and found 100 plants the owner said "he has a large number of marijuana smokers in his family".

COMMENT: Allowing the public to keep a marijuana plant for their own use is one way of cutting out the drug dealers. But sometimes some members of the public can take advantage of the situation. The humour is the obvious lie about the "large number of marijuana users in the family". Only Homer Simpson would come up with an excuse like that!

JOKE 199

Most drug dealers around the world are unemployed youths who want to "get rich quick". The only problem is "they get dead quick" once they start using the drugs.

COMMENT: This is Captain Hook logic. If you sell drugs you will "get rich" quickly. A good discussion point is this…. if you die from using drugs, that will be bad but you do get something better, you go to heaven! Add some funny comments and "see it" as drug dealers would.

JOKE 200

25 dope smokers were sitting on the beach. The first one said, "Look there's a boat", "No it's a barge", said the second one. "I don't think so. It's a Uboat", says the third one. "It

looks more like a seaplane", said the fourth. "No, it's a whale", says the fifth". "You people are stoned", says a "passer by".

COMMENT: Hallucinating can be a part of drug use "enjoyment". People around drug users will notice it very quickly…as the passer by pointed out. It is often very hard to deal with people under the "influence".

JOKE 201

A drug shop in the Netherlands is selling marijuana and other legal drugs. A foreign junkie came in and asked, "Have you got any cocaine?". "No, but we have Ocaine. It gives you the same trip without the hallucinations", said the shop keeper.

COMMENT: When New Zealand legalised synthetic drugs, there were a plethora of new drugs hitting the market. The joke here is about the "new drugs" creating the same effect as the "banned drugs"….yet they are legal.
The New Zealand Government probably realise that the legal drugs are going to create

the same problems they were trying to avoid…and banned them again.

JOKE 202

A certain Monarch punished one of his subjects to eternal poverty, destitution and stupidity for calling him a fool. According to his supporters, the monarch started the stupid joke and is simply suffering from "natural marijuana".

COMMENT: This is an imaginary joke about the "stupidity" of the State. It is also a satirical comment on the corruption of absolute power. I guess only Moe from "The Simpsons" can fit into such a role. In one episode he said that he was "eternally punished to be ugly" or something like that.

JOKE 203

It has been quoted in the New Zealand Herald that gangs are responsible for the distribution of drugs. The Black Power, Head Hunters, Skin Heads, Hells Angels, Mongrel Mobs and King Cobra. Spokespersons for all the gangs released statements denying the allegations. The King Cobra says they are simply trading copra, not drugs.

COMMENT: The gangs are the drugs dealers in New Zealand...according to the Police. This may be true as most gang members are drug users. The humour here is the attempt at disguising drug dealing as "copra trade". It is a bit of "Pacific humour".

JOKE 204

The Pacific region is becoming one of the most dynamic in terms of supplying fish to the world market. Many Pacific countries make millions of dollars selling fishing licences to multinational fishing companies. One Pacific Island Minister was quoted as saying "It's the only resource we have that is better than selling marijuana".

COMMENT: The Forum Fisheries Agency in Honiara, Solomon Islands is tasked with management or help manage the fish stock of the region. They sometimes help with selling "fishing licences" to multinational fishing companies for large sums of money. Probably because of the amount of fish they are allowed to take at a time. It is definitely much better than drug dealing.

JOKE 205

Commentators on the advance of technology say that after artificial diamonds the next will be artificial drugs. Every kind of drug will be designed to control all your emotions including "kissing monkeys". One wife has already ordered a drug to "stop her husband from excessive farting in church".

COMMENT: This is just a bit fantasy and humour. But it is true, if drugs are allowed to be sold in the shops, as in the case of New Zealand, the manufacturers will produce anything that customers demand.

JOKE 206

Drug dealers have come up with a brilliant idea. When they have a shootout with the Police, they will use "cocaine bullets" which will make the raid police high and abort the drug attack.

COMMENT: This is another bit of fantasy. Only Snake from "The Simpsons" will come up with a "brilliant idea" like that. Even Captain Hook will be capable of it, if he can use it against Peter Pan. This would be a super villains dream to have some "brain altering bullets" to use against their enemies.

JOKE 207

During the spread of Christianity in Europe in the 18th century, some Philosophers made the comment that it was the "Opium of the poor". One of the advantages of the opium of the poor is that you will not need any other drug to give you "that high".

COMMENT: It is true. I have met a lot of Christians who seem to have that "natural high". Maybe it is something the State can use on drug dealers and users who are difficult to rehabilitate. Almost like the common use of hypnotism against various ailments.

JOKE 208

Opium is a very good cash crop in some Middle Eastern countries. They supply multinational drug companies but are also being accused of supplying drug dealers.   A local spokesperson says that they have been smoking opium for centuries so what is the problem?

COMMENT: The humour here is the apparent confusion in certain Arab communities as to why Westerners disapprove of their opium use. After all, Westerners do smoke a lot of cigarettes…for the nicotine high. They also consume a lot of alcohol for its effect. Sometimes only Philosophers can understand and differentiate between traditional and cultural problems arising from such differences in views.

JOKE 209

Drugs are like beautiful women, says the bible. Once you fall for it, you will never recover. "That's right said one man, I have left my wife and married a monkey. At least I can leave anytime I want".

COMMENT: "If you are in love with a beautiful woman, watch your friends"…sang Dr Hook. The same goes for valuables like money, diamonds and so on. But it could also be the same with using drugs…it never ends. Like the man who married a monkey so he won't have to "worry about his friends"…perhaps using a less lethal form of entertainment might be the solution for drug users.

JOKE 210

Legendary blind USA singer Ray Charles was a constant user of drugs in his most productive years. It landed him in trouble with the authorities and his family. He did turn his life around and even got an apology from his home state of Georgia after banning him for speaking out against segregation. He was allowed back after 20 years. His song "Georgia" was made the State's official song. "The drugs did not break him but the ban nearly did" says a secret admirer.

COMMENT: The story of Ray Charles as told in his movie is a very inspirational yet brutally emotional with an underlying depressing effect. He became a superstar as a singer but was plagued by personal demons including drug use. I think the happy ending saved many people from being depressed watching it. It is an excellent "lesson" for drugs users to "learn" from his life.

JOKE 211

The USA Army is going to use drones to spy on drug dealers in the jungle of South and Central America. After one year they checked the videos and only found images of "wild animals mating".

COMMENT: This is just a bit of humour, but the point is that it could be a use for drones that maybe decommissioned after the "war on terror".

JOKE 212

The Speaker of Parliament in a Pacific Country was arrested by Police for "possession of drugs and firearms". He was later released and voted back to parliament because he was "only looking after the drugs and firearms for a neighbour".

COMMENT: This could be an episode from "Mrs Brown's Boys". The speaker of the Tongan Parliament was arrested by the Tonga Police and charged for possession of drugs and firearms. The drugs was said to be cocaine. He was later released and voted back to Parliament. People don't know whether to laugh or cry over this apparently....hilarious arrangement.

JOKE 213

The Mediterranean Shipping Company (MSC) lost its container ship the "Rena" in a recent disaster in Tauranga, New Zealand. The ship ran aground on a reef under suspicious circumstances. There was a rumour that it was carrying drugs. They only found "hundreds of containers filled with powdered milk".

COMMENT: This is just a joke. It is true there were "a lot of milk powder" on the boat but the obvious stupidity of the Captain or whoever landed the ship on the reef…can only be of comedy value.

JOKE 214

The Central Intelligence Agency (CIA) of the USA is spending billions of dollars fighting drug Cartels around the world. The only result is a more sophisticated drug distribution system which is harder to detect. A recent proposal suggest it would be cheaper if they just grow and sell them in the shops and put the drug dealers out of business.

COMMENT: It is rather ironic that the world's law enforcement agencies are just forcing drug dealers to be more sophisticated….when they can put them out of business by selling the stuff legally. One can only smile at such logic.

JOKE 215

Property bubbles in New Zealand are like Pyramid Schemes. You need more and more people to buy properties. When they run out of people, it collapses and everyone loses their money. Recently, there was a rumour that it is usually propped up with drug money. Then the "investor" grabs the money and "run" because he was being "caught out". COMMENT: This is just an imaginary joke. It is just poking fun at "property bubbles" in New Zealand where many people have lost large amounts of money when "the market collapses"….for whatever reason. It is a rather weird kind of investing. Putting lots of money into the property market and growing the bubble to benefit from it…but others lose large sums when it "burst".

JOKE 216

Drug Cartels are now investing in "clean businesses". It includes anything from contracting to franchising. In the restaurant business, they are rumoured to sell "marijuana flavoured ice-cream " and "cocaine" milk powder.

COMMENT: This is another imaginary joke. It will be good fun to discuss how many new products…with mind altering effects… that you can manufacture if it were legal.

I guess the point of legalising all hard drugs to destroy the drug trade has a lot of pros and cons.

JOKE 217.

A customer bought 17 books as Christmas gifts. The shop owner paid the writer only a third of the profits. The writer complained, it should be half. The shop Manager told him 'Sorry but we have to pay God as well'. The writer protested. 'But we don't have the same Gods, does that mean you have to pay for mine too?'.

JOKE 218

Drug Lords around the Pacific had a convention at the Lomoloma Hotel in Fiji. The Lord Chairman started the meeting with a prayer asking God to bless everyone and bless their "growing businesses".

COMMENT: This joke is just poking fun at people who use religion to hide their criminal activity. In many Pacific Islands, sometimes it is laughable what people ask God for and what they do in the name of religion.

You can drink alcohol, smoke cigarettes and still be considered a pillar of the community. Once you start smoking marijuana and use other drugs…you are frowned upon. But in other cultures like in the Middle East, for example, you can still smoke opium and be considered a responsible community leader. It may be a case of "cultural perspective" in some cases.

JOKE   219

News Broadcast.

'Apparently the much expected drop of 50,000 bales of ammunition and guns for the Allies , in the Middle East, has drifted into enemy territory'

JOKE 220

News Broadcast

'The Islamic State fighters were offended that their English was not understood by the target audience on television, according to a spokes person'.

JOKE 221

All the major religions believe in a better life after death, that is why Moslems blow themselves up so they can return to paradise sooner than expected.

JOKE 222

Europe has opened its doors for poor refugees from the Middle East. New Zealand and Australia should do the same by letting poor people from the Pacific enter their countries visa free.Unfortunately, Australia has started off on the wrong foot by deporting Kiwis after they lost the final in the last Rugby World Cup.

JOKE 223

Refugees to Paris should take heart from the current friction and ethnic isolation. That will give them time to set up some cells to sell their wares.

JOKE 224

Nostrodamus, the famous European prophet did predict that in the last days of the earth, there will be war among all countries of the world. At last count, most countries are already involved in the latest conflict in the Middle East.

JOKE 225

The United States has enough air power to continue shooting at the enemy on the ground, indefinitely, without committing, killing or injuring any of its troops. Now the Russians and the French have caught on to the idea.

JOKE 226

Syria is becoming a factory of terrorists says the French President. There are so many that some European countries are closing their borders.

JOKE 227

The Islamic State of Iraq and Syria (ISIS) has about 20 million supporters and access to $ 700 billion of potential funds for their war. It is the largest and most wealthy army in the world.

JOKE 228

Drones made for future wars are going to patrol the skies 24/7. All targets will be in their computers controlled by computers and personnel on the ground.

The next step will be drones thinking for themselves and going after the wrong people.

JOKE 229

Wars are so expensive to finance that most large companies around the globe try to have a piece of the action.

JOKE 230

The United States make most of its money

from arms export according to certain reports. The US Army also buys more arms than all of Europe put together.

JOKE 231

Africa was once the poor continent with millions of starving populations. Now they are joining the arms race even funding their own revolutions by selling some of the excess women to the highest bidders in the Middle East.

JOKE 232

The Turkish Kurds have won over one of the towns in Syria for the locals to return to their homes. The only problem is they have left for Europe and all the houses have been demolished from shelling the enemy.

JOKE 233

News broadcast

Russia joined the fight in Syria by bombing the United States supported rebels first.

JOKE 234

Islam believes in Jesus Christ but the Jews do not. That is one reason why they don't like Israel.

JOKE 235

Religious differences can be very sticky and difficult to overcome. Guns and bullets are often the only solution. However, in Russia, Moslems and Christians have been happily doing business for years and years. Money does talk.

JOKE 236

One solution to the overcrowding of refugees in Europe is to rebuild their homes in Syria and allow them to return, just like the Jews returned to Israel after World War II. It would be cheaper than trying to convert them to Europe's lifestyle.

JOKE 237

Certain very smart traders in the Middle East are selling arms to the rebels or anyone buying. Most of the guns have 'Property of the United States Army' printed on the barrel. They say it was their blessing like manna from heaven.

JOKE 238

One thing we can learn about the war in the Middle East. One side is getting richer while the other is getting new recruits. The best way to use untrained refugees is to train and arm them and send them back to liberate their country.

Joke 239

Why did the Chief kick the Chicken's ass? Answer: Because she does not have a front!

Joke 240

Chicken said to the Chief.

You idiot! That is not my ass you kicked. That was my tummy!

Joke 241

Why did the Chief kick the Chicken's tummy?
Answer: Because the tummy is too stupid.

Joke 242

A Chief and a Chicken walked along the road. Observers note, they look like twins.

Joke 243

Chief said to the Chicken.
'You are just a Chicken, I am the Chief".
Chicken replied, 'Do you like eating Chickens Chief?'.

Joke 244

Chicken announced at a Chicken meeting.
'We are going to rebel against the Chiefs, because they only want to eat pigs'.

Joke 245

Chicken announced at the next Chicken meeting.
'I am appointing myself Chief of the Chickens. We do not recognize any other Chiefs'.

Joke 246

Chief announced at the Chief's meeting.
'We will not recognize any Chickens. Chickens are only for lunch and dinner'.

Joke 247

Chicken announced at the Chickens meeting.
'I refuse to be called stupid because I will be turned into Chiefly food'.

Joke 248

Chief wrote to the Chicken.
'I forbid you to eat fish. I do not like eating Chickens that smell like fish'.

Joke 249

Chicken said to the Chief.
'You are just a coconut'.
Chief replied, 'No coconuts are trees'.

Joke 250

Chief said to the Chicken.
You are just a coconut. Chicken replied, 'No,
I am a Chicken'.

Joke 251

Chief said to the Chicken.
'You are not invited to our party'.
Chicken replied, 'I don't like male only
parties'.

Joke 252

Chicken gave the Chief the fingers. Chief said,
'That is not a finger, that is called a wing'.

Joke 253

Chicken announced at the Chicken's meeting.

'We Chickens are going to sabotage the
Chiefs Chicken farm by refusing to lay eggs'.

Joke 254

Chief said to the Chicken.
'I don't want my business in yours'.
Chicken replied, 'That's alright dear, its only
for laying eggs'.

Joke 255

Chickens protest against the cruelty of Chiefs.
The first banner read, 'Too many Chickens
die from Chiefly food'.

Joke 256

Chiefs meet in Parliament.
'We are going to ban all Chickens from
protesting. The world might find out our food
is no good'.

Joke 257

Chickens wrote to the United Nations.
'We are being banned by the Chiefs for

protesting against their poisonous food'.

Joke 258

Chiefs meet in Parliament.
'We are going to steal the Chicken's letter to the United Nations. The world might discover we are murdering the Chickens'.

Joke 259

Chickens protest again.
The first banner reads. 'Chiefs steal our mail'.

Joke 260

Chiefs meet in Parliament.
'We are going to ban pens and paper so Chickens cannot write letters to anyone'.

Joke 261

Chicken showed Chief her backside.
Chief said, 'Chicken, I only like colored feathers. Yours is all white'.

Joke 262

Chief and Chicken shared some dinner.
'What's yours Chief?', Chicken asked.
'A roasted male Chicken'. What's yours?'.
Chicken replied. 'A Chef's specialty'.

Joke 263

Chief was knocking on the door.
'Who's there?', called Chicken.
'The Big Bad Wolf'.
'Go away', cried Chicken. I only like to be
eaten by a bull'.

Joke 264

Chief asked Chicken out to lunch.
Chicken enquired. 'Would you like me to
come to your mansion? Or shall you come to
my tree?'.

Joke 265

Chief announced to the Chickens. 'From now
on, all Chickens are allowed to roam freely at
my mansion'.

Joke 266

Chicken got mad at the Chief.
'How dare you touch my breast?', she
shouted. 'Sorry, Chicken', Chief said. 'That is
just your feathers!'.

Joke 267

Chiefs had a banquet.
The menu was 'All Chicken in 10 course
meal'.

Joke 268

Chicken's protest at their ill treatment by the
Chiefs. The first banner read. 'Too many
Chiefs spoil the soup'.

Joke 269

Chickens had a meeting.
'From now on we will refuse to be Chief
entertainment. We only like to be Chief food'.

Joke 270

Chiefs announce in Parliament.
'Only wise Chickens are allowed to vote.
Stupid Chickens can cross the road'.

Joke 271

Chickens announce at their meeting.
'Why did we cross the road?'. All the
Chickens shouted. 'Because the Chiefs suck!'.

Joke 272

Chief and Chicken decide to have a truce.
Chief said, 'I agree to be your friend'.
Chicken agreed. 'You can have me anytime
Chief'.

JOKE 273

The South Pacific Commission celebrated the
opening of its new headquarters in 1994, in
Noumea, New Caledonia. One of the VIP
guests was asked by a journalist to comment
on the new building. He says, "Well it looks
like an upside down canoe".

JOKE 274

Fiji was kicked out of the commonwealth after the coup in 1999. When Suva locals were interviewed as to who started it, they said it was "A Tongan Guy".

JOKE 275

A certain organisation in the Pacific limits staff contracts to 6 years. When the Secretary General did 20 years, they said, "it's because some animals are more equal than others".

JOKE 276

In their efforts to draw global awareness to sea level rise and associated problems in the Pacific Islands, the small states proposed to establish the Pacific Island Small States Organisation or PISS.

JOKE 277

During its heyday the Nauru business statement listed $200 million invested in buildings, $10 million invested in infrastructure, $30 million invested in a jetplane and $2 million spent on bringing coconut fronds from the Phillipines for the Christmas celebrations.

JOKE 278

Part of the population of Kiribati was evacuated to Rabi Island in Fiji where they have flourished. Some people suggest if the sealevel rise any higher than the current "12 inches on the islands" they should also evacuate.

JOKE 279

The Ministry of Health in Tonga is promoting responsible drinking. They say that binge drinking is a problem. The local beer fans disagree. They say they are just being "consistent".

JOKE 280

The New Zealand Police recently arrested Tame Iti and members of the Tuhoe tribe. They were accused of planning to overthrow the Government with picks and shovels. They were also "learning terrorist activities and sleeping under trees".

JOKE 281

The FBI and the New Zealand Police confiscated goods and cash from the Kim.com mansion in Auckland. A figure of $200 million has been quoted in the news. $6 million has also been returned. However, the paper reports say the judges are not sure what the charges are.

JOKE 282

A certain Politician was kicked out of his village in Papua New Guinea. The village spokesman says he is not a Wantok. He is a Twotok.

JOKE 283

The Republic of Palau plans to invite Usain Bolt for "training sessions" with local sprinters, according to the local administrator, Paul Dee.

JOKE 284

French Polynesia is second only to Fiji in terms of income from tourism in the Pacific. Two gay men in Auckland plan to setup a kayak paddling business in Papeete to take advantage of the new wave of "new age" tourists.

JOKE 285

An Australian called a Tongan a coconut. The Tongan went to the Australian's house and counted 9 coconuts in his yard. Then he came back and said to him.... 'Sorry Boss, you have 9 coconuts in your yard, I only have bananas in mine'.

JOKE 286

In a recent newspaper report, the Republic of Marshall Islands has two problems. One is the traffic jam in the morning and evening on the one main road on the main island. The second is the problem of eating all the "stakes" donated by the Mormons.

JOKE 287

On a trip to Guam, a colleague said it took 2 hours to get from the airport to his hotel. The taxi driver says that "he drove around the long way to let him see the sights. A bit more expensive, but worth it", he says.

JOKE 288

Eight-eight millionaires had a conference in the Pacific Island of Tonga. 'Let's buy some of the islands and build hotels here to help the local economy', the Chairman said. So they bought 2 each. 'Mr Chairman', said the Secretary, 'Can we leave some islands for the King and his people?'. 'Yes, they can rent it from us', the Chairman replied.

JOKE 289

Australia is known as the "lucky" country. They have billions of dollars worth of minerals just waiting to be exported. The only drawback is that it is now the largest "asylum" in the world.

JOKE 290

A Professional working for one of the regional organisations asked his boss about his contract renewal one month from expiry. The boss said "he does not know anything". The staff member said "when the boss does not know anything, it's time to look for a new job".

JOKE 291

If you happen to travel to Samoa, visit the village of Falevao in Upolu. Stay overnight, eat as much as you can, elope with a local girl, and if you get caught, run like hell.

JOKE 292

The Pacific Ocean covers 33% of the earth, contains 22 Pacific nations and territories, 10 million people, 39 million coconuts and one university. The University of FSM.

JOKE 293

The Pacific Islands Tourism Association (PIFA) aims to promote the Pacific Islands as a tourist destination. The Naked Hotel in the Caroline Islands advertises "Don't bring anything, just your wallet".

JOKE 294

The Rarotongan Hotel in the Cook Islands is the cheapest in the region. It only cost $33 plus expenses for one night.

JOKE 295

A USA billionaire bought an island in Fiji for $US15 million then he sold it 10 years later for $US50 million. 'What did he do to develop the island?', asked a local Politician in Parliament. 'We did a survey and found lots of discarded bras and bikinis on the beach. Apparently, he is promoting, online, it as a treasure hunting island', answered the Tourism Chief.

JOKE 296

Toke Talagi, Prime Minister of Niue, wants the Forum countries to pay more attention to the regions fisheries resources. A local paper suggest
"selling more fishing licences to the Chinese to improve the management of migratory fishes".

JOKE 297

Pacific Islanders in Honolulu and mainland USA are well known for their "home handyman" skills. They can build fences, do driveways, prune trees, paint houses and use Mexicans as "free" labour.

JOKE 298

Gordon Ramsey is reported to start a cookery course in Sigatoka in Fiji soon. On the menu are curries, kokoda, luau, lovo and pawpaw pudingi.

JOKE 299

Pilots are famous and highly paid for their skill in transporting people around the Pacific. Recent suggestions to Air Pacific include, pilots should speak Hindi, dance the hula and perform mouth to mouth on any "pets" on board.

JOKE 300

Hugh Hefner proposed that the Playboy "Pet of the Month" should be its ambassador to the world. The latest addition to her travels is a tour of the Pacific to "mix with the locals". Her chores would include fishing with fishnets, weaving mats and "digging holes".

JOKE 301

The Pacific Island Seasonal Work Scheme in Australia and New Zealand has helped many island families financially. Up to 8,000 islanders are employed by the scheme each year. A recent enquiry in New Zealand found many employers only like Vanuatu employees because they don't complain, don't drink or smoke dope and they "always agree with the boss".

JOKE 302

Comedian Mike King was reported to have been "chased by a mob of his audience" in the city of   Tauranga in New Zealand because he "was making fun of   Kiwis".

JOKE 303

The Plumbers Association in Auckland got a frantic call from The Block TV programme to "unblock" their toilet during their last shooting session.

JOKE 304

Unemployed people in New Zealand are advised to "follow the money". That's why 4,000 are leaving to Australia every week.

JOKE 305

The late Dr 'Epeli Hau'ofa, Professor of Pacific Studies at the University of the South

Pacific, Fiji, in his comedy "Tales of the Tikongs" suggest that the "demise of village shops is directly correlated to local funerals" in the land of the Tikongs.

JOKE 306

One of the ancient Kings of Tonga had 200 wives, 100 concubines and he also 'recruits' all the pretty girls in the islands. 'What does he do with all these women?', asked one anthropologist studying history. 'I believe it was a breeding programme to increase the local population, often decimated by wars', answered the second anthropologist. 'If all the warriors have 50 wives each, that will keep them busy all year round that there is no need for wars!', observed the first anthropologist.

Joke 307

A self employed man in New Zealand filed his tax return for 2013. His tax deductible income was $195 for the whole year. A year later, he got a bill for $845.27 from the Accident Compensation Corporation. They have adjusted his income to $20,000 and charged him accordingly.

Joke 308

The Commonwealth Agricultural Bureau International (CABI) based in England started a project in the South Pacific to identify its fauna and flora. The project was accepted by donors with a budget of about $NZ 15 million in 1997. After 18 years there is still no sign of any activity. Apparently, the project was stolen by another organization!

Joke 309

A middle management Pacific Islander worked really hard with his staff and attracted $NZ 30 million in projects for his regional organization. After the first three years, the management decided to let him go because they need his $NZ30 million elsewhere in the organization.

Joke 310

The Boss of a certain Pacific regional organization assess his staff on their performance in the nightclubs rather than at work. His reasoning was that it's only when they get drunk he can see their real personality.

Joke 311

A certain regional organization in the Pacific hired its Boss, Finance Manager, Personnel Manager and Security Manager all from one country. After 3 years the organization crashed and all the money disappeared!.

Joke 312

A kid was punished by the leader of a certain Pacific country to live on the streets for the rest of his life. After 20 years he asked the kid what life on the street was like. The kid, being older and wiser, answered "I learned that you are just a mere mortal, when you die maggots will eat you".

Joke 313

The Tongan Police carried out a sting operation called "Rob Rob before he robs you". When they arrived at the village to question the locals, they were told that Rob had gone back to England but they recommend arresting Bob instead. So the sting operation was given a new name "The B operation".

Joke 314

Backside Whitelaw was the lawyer for Doddy Lahoya vs Soddy Lahoya over some real estate. However, the courtcase had to be postponed as Whitelaw was rushed to hospital to have his back side examined.

Joke 315

Constable 391 of Oklahoma City, USA, arrested John Wayne, Dean Martin and Clint Eastwood for fraud. The charges were for 'misleading the public in their latest movie'.

Joke 316

Racism within the New Zealand Police was investigated. The report suggested there is no racism within the Police but it recommended 'further education' for some of them.

Joke 317

The New Zealand Police blocked a certain criminal from getting a job for 18 years. It was later discovered that 200,000 children in New Zealand live in poverty because their parents cannot find jobs. The Government tried various employment projects and policy interventions only to find it was the Police Department that prevent people from working.

Joke 318

For many years, 95% of businesses in New Zealand fail within 2 years. The New Zealand Government gave the Ministry of Defence the task of protecting New Zealand Business. It was later revealed that foreigners and immigrants were deliberately sabotaging local businesses and stealing their ideas.

Joke 319

A certain Pacific Island was using its

diplomatic connections to punish its dissidents overseas. Their offences range from swearing at their esteemed leader, peeing on the Prime Minister's car and winking at the daughter of the local Governor.

Joke 320

A Policeman, who was well endowed, sired many, many children. When asked what the secret is. He says, "I give my female clients two options. One is a speeding ticket and second is a quickie. They always choose the second option for some reason".

Joke 321

The Mayor of a certain city in New Zealand went on a tour of China. During one important meeting, his wife rang on an urgent matter. She was told by the hotel receptionist "Sorry, his Excellency still in the course with our Mayoress".

Joke 322

A customer kept pulling a waitress's hair at a

restaurant. When the dessert menu was requested, the customer got a shock. The first dessert on the list was "Pull my pants down ice cream".

Joke 323

King Haku, a famous pro-wrestler in the USA, was formerly a sumo wrestler in Japan. He was very successful until he met Koo Stark, a pretty British model.

Joke 324

The problem with comedy these days is there are too many feckin comedians feckin swearing at each other, complained Mrs Brown.

Joke 325

The problem with politics these days is that there are too many feckin idiots in feckin positions of feckin power, complained Mrs Brown.

Joke 326

One man said to wife, "My dear, the problem is there are too many people who want to be me. I can count at least 3 people who are using my name. Wife replied, "Is that why I have 3 husbands?".

Joke 327

New World Order according to the news. 300 million Moslem Jihadists rule the world. 80% of army activity is to protect local business from bad creditors. 90% of taxi drivers have PhDs. 95% of Politicians did not go to school. Self-employed people earn less than the unemployment benefit.

Joke 328

A man went to holiday in the island of Tonga, South Pacific, every year and return a cripple every time. The Doctor told him it is gout made worse by the 'low antioxidant diet' he eats in Tonga. 'That includes stuff they put in your coffee and tea'. 'Like what?'....the man asked. 'You know, local water, sugar, milk and impurities!'.

JOKE 329

During the reign of the Tu'i Tonga (950-1865) many Tu'i Tongas were assassinated by warriors from other parts of the Empire. The Tu'i Tonga's security guards persuaded the Chiefs to crown a log of wood as the King. "They won't be able to assassinate him", they reasoned.

COMMENT: A humorous reference to one of the Tu'i Tonga's which was just a log of wood. There was an explanation for it but it maybe a diversion to prevent assassins from killing the real one. Whatever the reason it is certainly cause for a few smiles when you consider the subjects who talk and treat the log of wood like a King. For example, people saying "Good morning your majesty!" to the log of wood every morning!

JOKE 330

The Tu'i Tonga was well known for having many wives, sometimes more than 200 wives.

It inspired a dog breeding programme to advertise "males required to inseminate more than 200 females" in the local paper. More than 50,000 males in the Kingdom applied for the job, including some Ministers of the Crown.

COMMENT: The humor is in the confusion created by the ad. It did not mention they were female dogs.   The humor is also satirical ...aimed at the lack of sexual partners in Tonga despite the census showing female and male numbers are about the same. Tongan culture and Christianity frowns upon sex despite the obvious popularity of sex during the era of the Tu'i Tonga.

JOKE 331

After one funeral a Tongan man discovered all his tools, shopping, fridge, lawnmower and even his dog was missing. Enquiries found they were taken by his relatives "as payment for services rendered".

COMMENT: This is a standing joke in Tonga, when the relatives come to the funeral and after everyone leaves all the contents of the owners house are gone too. It used to be common that Tongans take whatever they like from a relatives house and forget to let him know they are borrowing his tools.

JOKE 332

During the Tongan Civil War, one Chief used to select his warriors by farting and asking them to assess the aroma. One warrior said, "It is fragrant like the flower of the ahi (sandalwood) tree". The Chief replied, "Great, you are the biggest liar in the land. I will use you as my master spy to spread rumours among the enemy".

COMMENT: It was a story that circulated in our area when I was young. The humor is satirical...an obvious reference to common people "greasing" or praising their Chief looking for a favour.

JOKE 333

After a prominent businessman died, he left all his wealth to his 3 children. To his last son, he left 3 rolls of toilet paper. It was the source of much mirth during the reading of the will until the first son went to the toilet. He came back and said, "There is no toilet paper". The last son said, "I will sell you a roll for $1 million". The first son said, "Great. You can sell me the other rolls as well".

COMMENT: The humor is the ridiculous heritage the youngest son got and his quick wit in selling the toilet paper for a ridiculously high price.

JOKE 334

A tourist was driving along Taufa'ahau Road, the main road on Tongatapu. A large sow and her piglets crossed the road   so she stopped and waited for them. One piglet decided to sit on the middle of the road and scratch her back. After 10 minutes the tourist decided to move it along by getting out and kicking it in the behind! She ran off squealing   into the bush. COMMENT: One of the disadvantages for tourism in Tonga are the free roaming pigs in the villages. The humor is satirical, aimed at the Tonga Tourism Industry being held up by free roaming pigs.

JOKE 335

Ghosts used to take over people's bodies in Tonga. The local Psychologist refer to it as " 'Avanga tukufakaholo" or "illness from the ancestors". "What do you call it when other ghosts take over?", a curious patient wanted to know. The Psychologist explained. "If it is a foreign ghost, we conclude that you are just crazy".

COMMENT: A satirical bit of humor about the local Psychologist and poking fun at how patients are diagnosed.

JOKE 336

A Tongan church goer wanted to go to heaven. He asked the Palangi Church Minister. The Church Minister said, "No, you cannot go to heaven, you are a sinner". The church goer said, "No my cousin the sina (iron rod)". "You have to repent first", the Church Minister said. "Sina, too strong", the Church goer concluded.

COMMENT: The humor is in the misunderstanding of the sound of the word sinner...which is also a local joke about an "erection". The local church goer says he cannot bend the "erection" its too hard.

JOKE 337

One villager was talking to another. "My brother tells me bullshit all the time. Last time he said he just came back from the moon". "That's nothing", said the other villager. "My brother tells me 1,000 stories every year, so far only one proved to be true".

COMMENT: A satirical joke about villagers telling tall stories. It is also an obscure funny reference to villagers taking pride in their family members travelling overseas. who are usually overstayers...'returning from the moon'.

JOKE 338

A fisherman was fishing one day. The God Maui appeared to him and asked whether he got anything. He said no. "Try throwing the line over there", Maui said pointing at the reef. After a while he got something and pulled it in. It was a bra. "No, that is not a fish. Try over there", Maui said pointing at another reef. After a while the fisherman got something and pulled it in. It was a G-String with an octopus attached to it. "Now, that is what I call fishing", Maui said.

COMMENT: A humorous story about ancient Gods and modern women...who like an octopus to be stuck in their 'G-string'.

JOKE 339

When Tonga won its first ever Olympic medal there was a parade in Nuku'alofa. A newspaper surveyed the people who attended to check local opinion. The conclusion was; "All the girls want to marry the Olympic Silver Medalist, all 10,000 of them!".

COMMENT: Poking humor at the tendency of local Tongan girls to like "high achieving" individuals....often from overseas....at the expense of the local boys.

JOKE 340

A study in Tonga found that 99.9% of the local population have very low IQs. Less than 10. The locals complained they don't know anything about the breeding habits of the Abominable Snowman on which the IQ test was based.

COMMENT: A satirical funny comment about the accuracy of IQ tests ...if performed on the local Tongans. Most individuals will not understand the questions....even though you would agree they are normal people.

JOKE 341

When the metric system was introduced to Tonga, they proposed 10 days per week and 10 months per year. During each week there will be 2 Fridays and 3 Saturdays because most people like to go out on Fridays and sleep in on Saturdays, and still work for 5 days!

COMMENT: A humorous swipe at the metric system with all measurements based in units of 10s or increments of 10s. For example, 10 mm per cm, 10x10 cm per metre, 1, 000 metre per kilometre, etc.

JOKE 342

A student in a local High School failed all 5 of his New Zealand School Certificate Exam subjects. His father asked him. "You should have passed all 5, we went through all the old exam papers and you knew all the answers". "Yeah, but I don't know how to write them down in English", was the reply.

COMMENT: One of the problems , in the past, with students in Tonga is their apparent inability to think and write in English.

JOKE 343

"The Royal Tongan Airlines flew a very good classy plane to Auckland and back but still failed as a business, what was wrong?", enquired the consultant. "Oh, the expatriate Managing Director was paid more than the annual profits, that was the problem", answered the local Manager.

COMMENT: A sarcastic comment about the failure of the Royal Tongan Airlines . There is also a deeper meaning behind it....about the failure of many Tongan Government ventures because of the gigantic salaries paid to expatriate experts to manage them.

JOKE 344

Boko Haram's plan for this conflict. 1. Steal as many women as possible and create a nation of his offspring with the hundreds of newly acquired wives 2. Send out his children to conquer the world

JOKE 345

Two villagers were talking. "Did you hear that Saddam Hussein had $999 million in his bank account?", one villager said. "Yeah, and the Americans stole it", said the other villager.

COMMENT: A Kava circle kind of joke. Tongan men drink kava, a Polynesian social drink made from the roots of the paper mulberry tree (*Piper methysticum*). There is a Tongan joke about the $999 million being a "fool's gold". The humor is that the Americans stole the "fool's gold". This joke is usually told when relatives from USA visit relatives in Tonga....just teasing their visiting brothers or cousins.

JOKE 346

39 Kings had a workshop. The first King said, "Let's degree that all the men in our countries be handsome". And it was done. "The second King said, "Let's degree that all the men in our countries be rich". And it was done. When it came to the 39th King's turn he said, "We only have one degree left but there are 2 items left on the agenda. One is to make all our women beautiful. Two is to make all our countries rich". The first King replied, "Don't worry about the monkeys let's make our countries rich".

COMMENT: This is an abstract kind of humor. Similar to the fool's gold, the number 39 in Tonga is also a joke about "fools". There is an ancient protocol in Tongan culture that anyone who is not a King or Chief is a fool or "vale". "Ha'ame'avale" refers to the general population who are not Chiefs or Kings.....it literally means they are all fools. The monkey reference is just a humorous   swipe at common women who are fools.

JOKE 347

A man was cooking Sunday 'umu lunch and he took a bit longer than normal. The wife rang on the cell phone to find out why it is taking so long. He said. "This is Masterchef Tonga. There is a hurricane on the way, everything is going wrong but lunch will be delivered as usual".

COMMENT: This is also a Kava circle type of humor. Obviously about cooking outside ('umu is an earth oven dug in the ground). The use of Masterchef is to enhance the ridiculous situation with cooking outside during a Hurricane....a sarcastic comparison of a posh kitchen and 'umu under a tree ....but somehow like Homer Simpson....everything goes wrong but the right results   are still   obtained.

JOKE 348

A taylor was selling her mumus at the cruise liner fair. A lady tourist came and asked her how much they were. "They are all $100 each", she said. "They are so cheap my dear. Why don't you sell me one for $500 and give me a receipt so I can show it to my neighbours when I get back?", she said.

COMMENT: A mumu is a long flowing floral dress down to the ankles with no belt. The humor is aimed at the locals tending to undersell their goods in the hope of making more money....and the tourist doing the valuation of the dress. A sarcastic remark at the "stupidity" of the locals.

JOKE 349

A young man just came back from New Zealand. His uncle asked him to buy him some shopping from town and gave him $20. "What is it you want?", the youngman asked. "Get me a carton of steinlager, a dozen bread, a dozen butter and jam, 2 strings of fish, a basket of yams and kumara, a Toyota cruiser and a bus and keep the change", the uncle said.

COMMENT: This is a common Tongan joke. ...about the locals teasing the relatives who come from overseas. Every visitor to Tonga from overseas...usually New Zealand, Australia and the United Sates of America are regarded as rich, by the locals.

JOKE 350

An expert Agricultural Marketing Group just returned to the Kingdom from overseas. They claim the market is flooded. The Minister asked why is it flooded. "Well, it's been raining the last 2 weeks   in Auckland for a start", said the leader.

COMMENT: One of the problems with Tongan agricultural exports in the past was the "lack of overseas markets" to sell Tongan produce. As it turned out, countries like Japan and Germany do not have problems with markets because they sell their own goods in the overseas markets rather than relying on anyone else to do it. The reference to "the market being flooded with water" is a local joke making fun of the experts who made the same excuse every time about their inability to sell Tongan produce overseas.

JOKE 351

A Church Minister was working in his plantation and God appeared to him. "You have been a good preacher. I will reward you by taking you to heaven in a chariot of fire". "But God, my children are still young who will look after them?", said the Minister. "Don't worry, your wife will marry again and the new husband will look after them". "In that case, I don't want to go to heaven, God", the Minster replied.

COMMENT: A joke poking fun at the enthusiasm shown by many Church goers to go to heaven but are very reluctant to "kick the bucket".

JOKE 352

A wife said to her husband. "I am going to this year's Christmas Party by myself". "Where's the Party dear?", the husband enquired. "At the Zoo". After the party the husband enquired, "How was the party dear?". "It was great, I was dancing with the occupants in the monkey room", the wife said.

COMMENT: Poking fun at clandestine marital affairs.

JOKE 353

A policeman gave chase to a car which overtook their van in a 65km/hr zone. When he got up with the car he accused the driver of driving at 80 km/hr. "How do you know I was driving at 80km/hr?", asked the driver. "We'll, you were going faster than us and we were doing 40 km/hr", the policeman said.

COMMENT: Poking fun at the "non-scientific methods" used by Police in Tonga. They are also accepted by the courts....which is even more hilarious. The Policeman forgot he was doing 40 km in a 65 km zone!

JOKE 354

One young man wanted to marry a pretty girl in the village. He brought her family gifts, took her to church, then got her pregnant. "What did you get pregnant for?", asked her father. "Dad, don't you want any grand-children?", she says.

COMMENT: A common occurrence in Tonga. Both young and old men "chasing" young women with gifts and cunning....but ironically the grandparents secretly enjoy the grandkids...without worrying about their origin.

JOKE 355

Two villagers were talking. "Our Chief is bigger than your Chief", the first villager said. "Are you sure?", said the second villager. "Yes", said the first villager. "He is even bigger than your car".

COMMENT: In recent times, in the Pacific, anyone who was overweight was highly regarded. It is a symbol of wealth and abundance. Sometimes villagers refer to their Chief as "large" to emphasize their importance, which is a source of humor for foreigners.

JOKE 356

A villager wanted to borrow some money from the Tonga Development Bank to start a plantation. The bank agreed to loan him $10,000 and using his 8 acre land as security but he has to start paying it back the next week. "Can you wait until the plantation is harvested and sold then I pay you?", he said. "No, it is bank policy", said the Bank Manager. "Can I borrow some more money in order to pay you while I wait for the plantation to mature?", the villager asked.

COMMENT: It is   a source of frustration for some growers in Tonga that they have to pay back their loan before the crop is harvested. The TDB requires a co-borrower with a job to start payments   a week after the loan is approved.

JOKE 357

King Nebuchadnezzar of Persia told his guards to throw Daniel in the Lion's Den for not following orders. Next morning the King was surprised that Daniel was standing beside the Lion padding its head. "What's that he said to the Lions?", he asked the Guard next to him. "I think he said, "Would you like to eat the King first or the guy on the left?".

COMMENT: A story from the bible. An exaggeration of God's power over   man and beast. Sometimes used in kava circles as a source of humor.

JOKE 358

A Reverend was giving a sermon in Church. "Our purpose in life is to seek the truth", he says. "You won't like the truth, shouted a drunk from outside. "And why is that young man?", the Reverend said. "Because I like being drunk, that's the truth!", he says.

COMMENT: A hilarious reference to the power of the "devil's water" (alcohol) over the youth of Tonga.

JOKE 359

Two boxers were talking. "I won my last fight", the first boxer said. "I knocked out the other guy". "I lost my last fight", the other boxer said. "I knocked out the referee".

COMMENT: A humorous reference to many boxers in Tonga, in the past, who have deliberately knocked out their opponents after the bell.

JOKE 360

A village comedian was always getting his laughs at the Kava Club by making fun of his relatives. One Uncle came to the Club one night and was not impressed. He told him off. The Village Comedian said, "Don't worry Uncle, it's better to be sillybrated than to be neglected".
COMMENT: Most Tongans are shy and will

not want to be the centre of attention. However, kids who have been overseas for a long time like to talk about their relatives and even make fun of them in public....but usually in a gentle "brotherly" way.

JOKE 361

A Kiwi went to Tonga for a holiday. He got a taxi from the airport to town and was charged $5,000. He said, "Don't worry, just put it on the bill". Then he got a hotel room and was charged $4,000 next morning. "Don't worry, just put it on the bill", he said. Then he went to town and a beggar asked him for $1 billion dollars. He said, "Don't worry, just put it on the bill". "Who do I send the bill to, Sir?", the beggar asked. "Bill Gates", the Kiwi replied.

COMMENT: Just a silly joke about the poor dreaming of being rich.

JOKE 362

A drunk was staggering through a village. "Anyone in this town want to fight?", he shouted. "No one can beat me in a fist fight", he shouted again. Then his pants fell down and he was holding it with one hand. A bold little boy stepped forward. "Yes, I will challenge you to a fist fight". "Why didn't you challenge me when I had 2 hands?", the drunk complained.

COMMENT: A funny reference to the silly antics of drunks in the villages.

JOKE 363

A very bright and able student, in a local University in Tonga, kept failing his Chemistry subject. His father asked him, "What is the problem?". "I don't like being a Mystery", he says.

COMMENT: A bit of humor about excuses at failing exams. There is also a deeper meaning about games, doubles and deception.

JOKE 364

A local newspaper was trying to train some new journalists. They were taught how to be good critics. They have to be witty, creative and original. When the final exam paper was collected, the examiner looked at the first entry in the creative criticism section, "Criticizing cows for burning the milk", it said.

COMMENT: A silly reference to the desire of some village comedians to be original with the result being more hilarious than intended. A parallel of "farting cows causing global warming".

JOKE 365

The Psychologist said to the patient, "So what do you want to do next year?". "We'll, I am sick of being crazy. I want to be smart next year", he says.

COMMENT: A bit of humor about some people who are just "crazy on purpose". But also the patients total reliance on the Doctor....that is...that Doctors can make them smarter!.

JOKE 366

A famous writer gave some books to a few shops to trial. After six months he checked and they were all gone. Upon further enquiries they emailed him, "No Sales". The books were not returned either. Next day he emailed them "All right, you can have lunch on me".

COMMENT: Just a silly comment about retail sales and the cost of doing business. The meaning of course, is that the retailer has spent the money.

JOKE 367

A writer was talking to a villager. "So you haven't got a job in 50 years? But you educated 7 grown up children? You prepare a feast for the Church 4 times a year? You donate $1,000 to the Church every year? You have a large, furnished and beautiful house? You have a new Toyota cruiser? You travelled overseas many times? How do you do it? "We'll, I always believed that God will provide and he has", said the villager.

COMMENT: It is a source of humor for foreigners who assess Tongan villager's income. They seem to be rather wealthy with no obvious income.

JOKE 368

"Flies perform a good service in our community. They eat all the leftover foods and rubbish and convert them into soil", the teacher said. "So why do people hate flies?", the student ask. "I guess they sometimes shit on your food if they land on it. Not exactly the right place to drop some soil", the teacher said.

COMMENT: A humorous comment about the abundance of flies in Tonga. During one year when the squash export failed and thousands of tonnes were left to rot in farms....millions of flies invaded the villages of Tongatapu.

JOKE 369

A PhD graduate just returned from overseas. There was much jubilation among the relatives. "He should be a Doctor at the hospital", said one. "No, he is crazy he can't speak Tongan properly, he should be a teacher", said another. "Why don't   we get him a wife first?", said a third. "Our new Church Minister is a woman and hasn't got a husband yet", she suggested. When the young man heard their plans he was on the next plane out of the country.

COMMENT: Poking fun at overseas graduates and how their Tongan relatives make plans for them.

JOKE 370

Squash was a very successful export commodity for Tonga. There was a plan to make baby food from the tonnes of discarded squash in the field after exports. They were left to rot in the fields and bred millions of flies. Locals refer to it as the "Baby Fly Project", baby flies eating the baby food. COMMENT: Many of the plans to add value to the successful squash project were shelved and squash fruits rot in the fields by the thousands.

JOKE 371

The God Tangaroa came down from the sky and saw a beautiful woman sunning herself on a beach on Tongatapu. The woman saw him and asked, "Who are you?". "I am Tangaroa, Lord of the Sky", he said. "Is that why your tongue is hanging down at your knees?", asked the woman.

COMMENTS: A humorous comment about sex in ancient times.

JOKE 372

One man walked into a supermarket and asked the female staff. "Anyone wanna sleep?".The Store Manager came. "What seems to be the problem?". Man asked if he can sleep on the floor!

JOKE 373

Lady to Lord. "Wanna sleep tonight?". Lord replied, "How about tomorrow?". Lady checked her schedule. "Sorry not available".

"How about we sleep everyday? Can't go without sleep for more than 16 hours", Lord replied.

JOKE 374

Teacher to class of 14 year olds. "Anyone here didn't sleep last night?". The whole class put up their hands. "How about the previous 2 nights?", Teacher asked again. The whole class put up their hands, again.

JOKE 375

Boss to Secretary. "I didn't have much sleep in the last week. I'm going to have a lie down in the clinic rest room". Secretary suggested. "Want me to sleep with you?".

JOKE 376

King to Queen. "Tonight is the night". Queen says, "Yes the knight is well hung". King to Queen. "Yes, I hung him yesterday".

JOKE 377

TV Commentator. "The sleeping wave is sweeping everyone off their feet. They sleep in cars, bedrooms, chairs, swimming pools, in the sea, aeroplanes, boats and guess what? In the toilets as well!".

JOKE 378

Male Police Officer to Female Driver. "I stopped you because you were sleeping at the wheels". Driver said, "Sorry, I can't sleep with the wheel. How about you?".

JOKE 379

Keffai said to Kekkai. "Wanna eat me?". Kekkai said, "Wanna sleep me?". Keffai slapped Kekkai in the face.

JOKE 380

Mayor to Mayoress. "Can you announce to our staff there will be no sleeping on the job tolerated?". "Don't worry dear, they sleep at lunch time", Mayoress advised.

JOKE 381

Male Journalist writes. "Sleeping is such sweet solace, except when the woman refuses".

JOKE 382

William Shakespeare. "To sleep or not to sleep that is the question. Whether tis nobler in the mind to face a naked woman or to take up arms and face a sea of naked women and by opposing get slapped in the face by all of them".

JOKE 383

"I am sleeping tonight", says Tom to a friend.
"Who are you sleeping with?", friend asked.
"No one, it's much better", Tom says.
If no one is that good can I have her for a night?", friend asked.
"You can have no one for as long you want mate", Tom offered.

JOKE 384

During the reign of the Tu'i Tonga (950-1865)

many Tu'i Tongas were assassinated by warriors from other parts of the Empire. The Tu'i Tonga's security guards persuaded the Chiefs to crown a log of wood as the King. "They won't be able to assassinate him", they reasoned.

COMMENT: A humorous reference to one of the Tu'i Tonga's which was just a log of wood. There was an explanation for it but it maybe a diversion to prevent assassins from killing the real one. Whatever the reason it is certainly cause for a few smiles when you consider the subjects who talk and treat the log of wood like a King. For example, people saying "Good morning your majesty!" to the log of wood every morning!

JOKE 385

The Tu'i Tonga was well known for having many wives, sometimes more than 200 wives. It inspired a dog breeding programme to advertise "males required to inseminate more than 200 females" in the local paper. More than 50,000 males in the Kingdom applied for the job, including some Ministers of the

Crown.

COMMENT: The humor is in the confusion created by the ad. It did not mention they were female dogs.   The humor is also satirical ...aimed at the lack of sexual partners in Tonga despite the census showing female and male numbers are about the same. Tongan culture and Christianity frowns upon sex despite the obvious popularity of sex during the era of the Tu'i Tonga.

JOKE 386

After one funeral a Tongan man discovered all his tools, shopping, fridge, lawnmower and even his dog was missing. Enquiries found they were taken by his relatives "as payment for services rendered".

COMMENT: This is a standing joke in Tonga, when the relatives come to the funeral and after everyone leaves all the contents of the owners house are gone too. It used to be common that Tongans take whatever they like from a relatives house and forgets to let him know they are borrowing his tools.

JOKE 387

During the Tongan Civil War, one Chief used to select his warriors by farting and asking them to assess the aroma. One warrior said, "It is fragrant like the flower of the ahi (sandalwood) tree". The Chief replied, "Great, you are the biggest liar in the land. I will use you as my master spy to spread rumours among the enemy".

COMMENT: It was a story that circulated in our area when I was young. The humor is satirical...an obvious reference to common people "greasing" or praising their Chief looking for a favour.

JOKE 388

After a prominent businessman died, he left all his wealth to his 3 children. To his last son, he left 3 rolls of toilet paper. It was the source of much mirth during the reading of the will until the first son went to the toilet. He came back and said, "There is no toilet paper". The last son said, "I will sell you a roll for $1 million". The first son said, "Great. You can sell me the other rolls as well".

COMMENT: The humor is the ridiculous heritage the youngest son got and his quick wit in selling the toilet paper for a ridiculously high price.

JOKE 389

A tourist was driving along Taufa'ahau Road, the main road on Tongatapu. A large sow and her piglets crossed the road   so she stopped and waited for them. One piglet decided to sit on the middle of the road and scratch her back. After 10 minutes the tourist decided to move it along by getting out and kicking it in the behind! She ran off squealing   into the bush.

COMMENT: One of the disadvantages for tourism in Tonga are the free roaming pigs in the villages. The humor is satirical, aimed at the Tonga Tourism Industry being held up by free roaming pigs.

JOKE 390

Ghosts used to take over people's bodies in Tonga. The local Psychologist refer to it as " 'Avanga tukufakaholo" or "illness from the ancestors". "What do you call it when other ghosts take over?", a curious patient wanted to know. The Psychologist explained. "If it is a foreign ghost, we conclude that you are just crazy".

COMMENT: A satirical bit of humor about the local Psychologist and poking fun at how patients are diagnosed.

JOKE 391

A Tongan church goer wanted to go to heaven. He asked the Palangi Church Minister. The Church Minister said, "No, you cannot go to heaven, you are a sinner". The church goer said, "No my cousin the sina (iron rod)". "You have to repent first", the Church Minister said. "Sina, too strong", the Church goer concluded.

COMMENT: The humor is in the

misunderstanding of the sound of the word sinner...which also an local joke about an "erection". The local church goer says he cannot bend the "erection" its too hard.

JOKE 392

One villager was talking to another. "My brother tells me bullshit all the time. Last time he said he just came back from the moon". "That's nothing", said the other villager. "My brother tells me 1,000 stories every year, so far only one proved to be true".

COMMENT: A satirical joke about villagers telling tall stories. It is also an obscure funny reference to villagers taking pride in their family members travelling overseas., who are usually overstayers...'returning from the moon'.

JOKE 393

A fisherman was fishing one day. The God Maui appeared to him and asked whether he got anything. He said no. "Try throwing the line over there", Maui said pointing at the reef.

After a while he got something and pulled it in. It was a bra. "No, that is not a fish. Try over there", Maui said pointing at another reef. After a while the fisherman got something and pulled it in. It was a G-String with an octopus attached to it. "Now, that is what I call fishing", Maui said.

COMMENT: A humorous story about ancient Gods and modern women...who like an octopus to be stuck in their 'G-string'.

JOKE 394

When Tonga won its first ever Olympic medal there was a parade in Nuku'alofa. A newspaper surveyed the people who attended to check local opinion. The conclusion was; "All the girls want to marry the Olympic Silver Medalist, all 10,000 of them!".

COMMENT: Poking humor at the tendency of local Tongan girls to like "high achieving" individuals....often from overseas....at the expense of the local boys.

JOKE 395

Maui, a Polynesian God, liked a Princess he saw from the sky. However, when he came down to see her she was getting married to a handsome young man. Maui was not to be discouraged, he changed the young man into a fish and took the Princess with him to the sky.

JOKE 396

A study in Tonga found that 99.9%   of the local population have very low IQs. Less than 10. The locals complained they don't know anything about the breeding habits of the Abominable Snowman on which the IQ test was based.

COMMENT: A satirical funny comment about the accuracy of IQ tests ...if performed on the local Tongans. Most individuals will not understand the questions....even though you would agree they are normal people.

JOKE 397

When the metric system was introduced to

Tonga, they proposed 10 days per week and 10 months per year. During each week there will be 2 Fridays and 3 Saturdays because most people like to go out on Fridays and sleep in on Saturdays, and still work for 5 days!

COMMENT: A humorous swipe at the metric system with all measurements based in units of 10s or increments of 10s. For example, 10 mm per cm, 10x10 cm per metre, 1, 000 metre per kilometre. etc.

JOKE 398

A student in a local High School failed all 5 of his New Zealand School Certificate Exam subjects. His father asked him. "You should have passed all 5, we went through all the old exam papers and you knew all the answers". "Yeah, but I don't know how to write them down in English", was the reply.

COMMENT: One of the problems , in the past, with students in Tonga is their apparent inability to think and write in English.

JOKE 399

"The Royal Tongan Airlines flew a very good classy plane to Auckland and back but still failed as a business, what was wrong?", enquired the consultant. "Oh, the expatriate Managing Director was paid more than the annual profits, that was the problem", answered the local Manager.
COMMENT: A sarcastic comment about the failure of the Royal Tongan Airlines . There is also a deeper meaning behind it....about the failure of many Tongan Government ventures because of the gigantic salaries paid to expatriate experts to manage them.

JOKE 400

Two villagers were talking. "Did you hear that Saddam Hussein had $999 million in his bank account?", one villager said. "Yeah, and the Americans stole it", said the other villager.

COMMENT: A Kava circle kind of joke. Tongan men drink kava, a Polynesian social drink made from the roots of the paper mulberry tree (*Piper methysticum*). There is a

Tongan joke about the $999 million being a "fool's gold". The humor is that the Americans stole the "fool's gold". This joke is usually told when relatives from USA visit relatives in Tonga....just teasing their visiting brothers or cousins.

RAINBOW ENTERPRISES BOOKS

If you enjoyed interactive humor visit amazon kindle to view some of our other ebooks on humor by James Boss.

Rainbow Enterprises also supply books on Pacific science, environment, stories and poetry.

If you are interested in religion try some of our books on science and religion called 'God is Energy. Do you Believe? There are four of them.

Or checkout the kindle countdown deals and free ebooks!

There is something there for everyone!

www.ingramcontent.com/pod-product-compliance
Lightning Source LLC
LaVergne TN
LVHW051122080426
835510LV00018B/2182